The Random Thoughts of a Christian Parrot

Coco

Fat Parrot Press

This First Edition published in the UK by

The Fat Parrot Press
Parkstone
George Nympton
Devon
EX36 4JE

British Library Cataloguing in Publication Data
Data available

Hardback ISBN: 978-1-5272-9810-1

Designed and typeset by
GreenGate Publishing Services, Tonbridge, Kent

Illustrations by
Russell Parry and Sue Swales;
Kriszti Alapi and Mathieu Labrosse

Printed and bound in Great Britain by Bell & Bain Ltd, Glasgow

Coco writes a weekly blog which is read in more than
40 countries around the world. You can find it by googling

Christianparrot.com/Random Thoughts of a Christian Parrot

A free subscription service is available.

Contents

Dedication

This book is dedicated to the memory of David Campbell who features in the following pages on two separate occasions. For more than ten years David defied the odds, battling against extraordinary adversity as his health declined. He rarely complained or asked 'Why me?' He approached each day with a smile on his face and lived life as fully as his health permitted. He showed us all how to live a life well and inspired everyone who knew him through his unshakable Christian faith.

Our loss is very much Heaven's gain.

Foreword

The Right Reverend Jackie Searle
Bishop of Crediton

How do we view events in the world and changes in our society? How do we know what really matters? And how do we find faith in this sometimes funny, sometimes troubling, beautiful world of ours? Coco the Christian Parrot offers 'Random Thoughts' that together offer reflection, food for thought, guidance and imagination, pointing us to notice God in our midst. The mix of humour, challenge, biblical text and photography, along with the views of our perceptive parrot, make this book a unique reflection on our twenty-first century lives. I commend it to you.

Bishop Jackie

Acknowledgements

I would like to acknowledge and thank the following humans for enabling me to publish this book.

My human owner Richard Holloway who has taken on the role of typist and publicist.

The human family where I live for putting up with both my human owner and myself over so many years.

Sheila Moston, based in Woolacombe, Devon, an avid reader of my blogs who first gave me the idea of turning them into a book.

Kriszti Alapi and Mathieu Labrosse, based in Montreal, Canada for their hours of patience and creativity with the Photoshop work in this book.

Russell Parry and Sue Swales, based in Shrewsbury, Shropshire, for their drawings.

David Mackin based in Tonbridge, Kent for his typesetting and design work.

Finally, my very special thanks go to the Revd. David Baker based in North Molton, Devon for welcoming me into the parish team, and accepting that a parrot can preach the Christian message just like anyone else. Without David supporting me with my original weekly blog, this book would never have materialised.

Preface

Reverend David Baker
Edgemoor Group of Parishes, North Devon

It's not every day that a parrot publishes his own book. But Coco, the Senegal Parrot is not your everyday kind of bird. He's the first parrot I know to write a weekly Christian blog which has now been read in more than 40 countries around the world. And during the last 12 months, he's been a regular feature in the weekly Zoom Services held by the Edgemoor Group of Parishes in North Devon. So this is a parrot of some pedigree.

The Random Thoughts of a Christian Parrot views the world through the eyes of a parrot, lifting the reader out of their normal human perspective. In my experience, seeing life from a new perspective is half the battle in bringing people to the Christian faith. Coco's messages are very simple and straight-forward but they help us to focus on what we may have missed or forgotten. His writings are full of relevant quotations from the likes of Albert Einstein, Mother Teresa, Corrie ten Boon and Captain Sir Tom Moore. And his messages mix humour with current events, science with the wonder of creation, and relevant issues such as difference and diversity. Every message is underpinned by Biblical text.

This is a book for dipping into; each message is rather like a 'parrot thought for the day'. I hope you enjoy reading it as much as I have.

Reverend David Baker

A Cathedral of Love?

I know I've said it before, but I'll say it again. Parrots are vain! Obsessed with having beautiful feathers. And quite a few humans are exactly the same....

We can all fall into the trap of judging everything by its immediate physical form. We get sucked in by the allure of beauty, image, wealth, success and 'celebrity status'. We can take everything around us at 'face value'. But what really lies behind the façade?

I know of a very disabled human man who's in constant pain. He needs crutches and a wheelchair to get around. So if you placed him next to this year's 'Mr. Universe', who would you be more drawn to?

And then there's dear old Nanna who lives on the other side of our house. She's getting rather frail and forgetful. Put her next to the current World Quiz Champion. Who would you find more interesting to talk to?

Or what about some small parrot that exists in a rusty old cage, or a human struggling to make ends meet, who survives in a tiny bedsit? Line them up beside a self-made millionaire who resides in a giant mansion. Who would grab your interest first?

2

In God's world, nothing is quite as it seems. The human in the wheelchair is really a saint because of all the things he's done for others in his life, despite his sufferings and disability.

And Nanna might not be so good at quizzes these days. But she still shines as a beacon of goodness and generosity towards others.

And what about that rusty parrot cage and the tiny bedsit? Well, they are really 'cathedrals of love' because their occupants have allowed them to become filled with the presence of Jesus.

So do we simply take everything at face value? Or do we look a bit deeper? Jesus talked about the people who…

Though seeing, they do not see *and* … though hearing, they do not hear or understand.   (Matthew 13:13b).

So often, it's those people and things that we don't immediately notice, that really count for everything.

A Choir of Angels

A great joy of living in the countryside is waking up in the Springtime to the sound of the dawn chorus. My feathered friends put on a wonderful performance every single morning. Intricate songs, chirrups, tweets, warbles, drumming, staccato and vibrato; – every different contribution blending into the most beautiful harmony which celebrates life and the new day ahead. A day of opportunity, purpose and hope.

And what makes the dawn chorus all the more special is that rivals sing together with rivals. Competitors with competitors. And different species with different habits and colours forget about their differences and come together to create a glorious natural harmony. It gives us all a glimpse of what might be, of what could be here on Earth, and what will be in Heaven.

Unity, fellowship and harmony succeeding over self-interest, prejudice, and rivalry. There are times when all humans need to have a 'dawn chorus' within their families, their communities, in the midst of their work and within their politics. And certainly between their different nations. So that they focus on similarity rather than difference. They build bridges instead of walls. And seek unity rather than isolation.

Sometimes it can take God's natural world to show humanity the obvious. And to make the words of the Bible come to life.

Live in harmony with one another.   (Romans 12:16)

Finally, all of you, live in harmony with one another; be sympathetic, love as brothers, be compassionate and humble.   (1Peter 3:8)

There is neither Jew nor Greek, slave nor free, male nor female, for you are all one in Christ Jesus.
                                      (Galatians 3: 28)

All Shall Be Well ...

How quickly things can change in life. Especially if you're a human being. Because humans have all kinds of sophisticated systems and mechanisms and customs that usually allow them to control their existence. But suddenly, everything's in disarray. For a great many humans, work has stopped. Schools have shut. People must stay indoors. Supermarket shelves are bare. Hugs, kisses and handshakes are banned. And for many, money – that primary driving-force in human life – has become very scarce. In the short-term at least, humanity is no longer in control of its destiny. And so a great many people are frightened. Very frightened indeed.

And yet, in some ways, nothing's really changed. Because none of us have ever had real control over our final destiny. It's just that we liked to think we had. Daily systems, routines, and modern technology have offered comfort and some security, but they have also served as rather flimsy 'wrappers' hiding the fact that we all remain vulnerable. Vulnerable to illness, hard times, and ultimately to death itself. Humanity has never been as self-sufficient as it liked to believe. And in these terrible times of Coronavirus, this is especially true for the elderly, the weak, the vulnerable and the sick.

But you know, this is also a time when the words of Jesus can come to life in our lives. Perhaps more vividly than ever before. Because time and time again in the Gospels, Jesus reminds us all that we are never abandoned during our times of suffering, and that we all have the promise of Heaven:

And it seems that the tougher our existence here upon Earth, the more our case is prioritised in Heaven.

> So the last will be first, and the first will be last.
> (Matthew 20:16)

Blessed are you who are poor, for yours is the kingdom of God. Blessed are you who hunger now, for you will be satisfied. Blessed are you who weep now, for you will laugh.
(Luke 6: 20–21).

When Jesus encountered the Samaritan woman at the well, He told her that her water would only sustain her for a day. But His 'Living Water' would sustain for eternity:

> Jesus answered: 'Everyone who drinks this (well) water will be thirsty again, but whoever drinks the water I give him will never thirst. Indeed, the water I give him will become in him a spring of water welling up to eternal life.
> (John 4:13)

We will always have to ride out challenges and storms during our time here on Earth. And some of them, like the Coronavirus epidemic, won't be easy. But because Jesus died on the cross for every one of us, we have all been given the ultimate insurance policy of a wonderful existence in Heaven should we choose to accept it.

In a parrot nutshell, Jesus gives us all a light at the end of the tunnel. In the words of the medieval theologian, Julian of Norwich [born 1342]:

All shall be well. All shall be well. Every manner of things shall be well.
(Julian of Norwich from: *Revelations of Divine Love*: Boston USA: Digireads.com [2013])

A Million Tiny Fireballs of Light

Not all parrots go to sleep when nightfall comes. While my human family are happily slumbering in their beds upstairs, I sometimes open up an eye and gaze out through the window at the stars above. On a clear, frosty night, I look out in wonder as a million tiny fireballs of light sprinkle their warmth and glow across the dark velvet of the night sky. And the sheer scale and immensity of it all can make me feel very small.

After all, being a small parrot, I occupy a pretty small space within the entirety of the universe. I may be loud and brightly coloured, but in the whole scheme of things, I'm rather insignificant. Humans might not look twice at me, because parrots don't run the country, (although it would probably be a lot better if they did). And parrots aren't very good for the economy because they gnaw through most of their assets.

So if I'm not important in the human world, and I'm a tiny blip within the universe, how can I ever be important to God? And yet, somehow – like everybody else – I am. Because we are all a part of God's creation, and we all have the potential to be used for God's purpose. Even if that's in some miniscule way.

You see, we're all rather like those stars in the sky. We all have a certain life and energy about us. Some more than others. And while we have life here on Earth, we can use whatever we have for the work of God. Because God doesn't just use 'special' folk for His work. Instead, He will use anyone that offers themselves up to Him. Our apparent insignificance doesn't matter. All we're asked to do is say 'yes' to God when we receive a prompt.

For humans, that might mean that you preach from the church pulpit, or organise the flower rota, or host a prayer group, or simply welcome people as they arrive at church. It may mean that you are honest and compassionate at your place of work or college, or that you give up time to help your elderly neighbours, or that you buy a sandwich for a down-and-out. Or you might even be a parrot that tries to write a Christian book!

By answering 'the call,' and doing something for God, you are becoming part of a collective whole. Like one of those tiny, seemingly insignificant stars in the night sky, which together with a million others, transforms the all-consuming darkness into a beautiful, living, spiritual wonder. We can all be 'fireballs of energy' for God, even when we're old or feeling weak. Because we all have an inner light to shine.

To this end I labour, struggling with all His energy, which works in me.   (Colossians 1:29).

… shine like stars in the universe … .   (Philippians 2:15b)

I can do everything through him who gives me strength.
                                         (Philippians 4:13)

A Parliament of Parrots?

I always think that humans outdo even parrots when they gather together in their parliament buildings and squabble. Talk about a cacophony! It can be complete chaos with shrieks, jeers, whistles and all kinds of noises that even a parrot wouldn't dream of making.

In the British House of Commons, there's one poor chap that only knows one word, and he yells it out incessantly. 'Order, order, order!' A bit of a one trick pony, if you ask me. Surely someone, somewhere could teach him a few other words to say?

Meanwhile, the pompous, self-righteous squawks and self-adulation carry on, interspersed by aggressive attacks on the opposition. It's enough to give any half-decent parrot a splitting headache!

And do the words that are said actually mean anything? Promises, justifications, explanations, false expressions of outrage and indignation that toe the party line…. How often is it all a load of froth that amounts to nothing worthwhile?

The words that we speak, the tone in which we say them, and the sincerity of our message, are all vitally important. Because our words can be very powerful. They can lead to trust or distrust; unity or discord; togetherness or separation; love or hatred; peace or conflict; a common sense of purpose or total anarchy.

Jesus was always very measured in everything that He said. No careless word ever left His lips. He didn't inflame situations through the choice of His words or the tone in which He said them. Some people rejected His message, but never His actual words.

If only humans could be the same. Because they get it wrong all the time. Not only in the House of Commons or the U.S. Senate, but in all walks of life. Uncontrolled emotion, self-righteousness, a lack of tact, bull-headedness – they all ultimately lead to conflict and strife.

Maybe Parliament would be a much better place if it was run by a load of parrots. Just imagine it. The Cockatories. The Big Beak Democrats. The Green Amazon Party. The African Grey Socialists. All in one big feathery coalition, harmonised at the core by the inclusion of The Love Bird Party. With mutual preening and nut-sharing before every Parliamentary session!

Maybe this is just a pipedream, but always remember that there are better ways of doing things. And that applies to all walks of life. Sometimes we simply need to be stopped in our tracks and look outside the box to see things differently. To see how our words and actions impact on the world around us. And ask ourselves what we can do to make things better. How would Jesus have gone about things?

For by your words you will be acquitted, and by your words you will be condemned.   (Matthew 12: 37)

A gentle answer turns away wrath, but a harsh word stirs up anger.   (Proverbs 15:1)

Are We Really So Clever?

There's a tendency amongst some parrots and humans for us to believe that we're cleverer than we really are. And there are occasions in life when something occurs to knock us down a peg or two; to deflate our puffed-up egos. And I recently came across a story on the internet which demonstrates this rather well.

A magician, working on a cruise ship, had a pet parrot that would constantly ruin his act. The bird would call out to the audience: 'He's got the card up his sleeve', or 'It's in his pocket', or 'He's got two cards the same!' The parrot thought he was being extremely clever, until one day, there was a massive explosion, and the ship sank. The parrot and the magician – both dazed and bruised – found themselves floating on a piece of wreckage together. The parrot simply stared at the magician for four long days before finally saying: 'Okay. I give up. What did you do with the ship?'

The parrot didn't know quite as much as he thought. And the same is true of many humans. They can fly planes in the sky, and rockets to Mars. They put up buildings that can be half a mile high. They connect the world through the magic of the internet. But despite all this, they can't create life, and they can't prevent death. They can tinker with what's before them, but they can't assume ultimate control of it.

So it's very important for us to show some humility as we go about our daily lives. Because ultimately, we're not in charge. And we never will be. And we're not as clever as we like to believe. Yes, human science and technology have taken enormous strides in recent times. But nothing's really changed. Countless generations have shared a common arrogance. Which is why so much is written about humility in the Bible.

> When pride comes, then comes disgrace, but with humility comes wisdom.   (Proverbs 11:2)
>
> Seek the Lord, all you humble of the land, you who do what he commands, Seek righteousness, seek humility … .   (Zephaniah 2:3)
>
> … show true humility towards all men.   (Titus 3:2)

In God's eyes, humility is every bit as important as love and righteousness. So for the rest of today, I'd better get off my highest perch and sit somewhere lower down!

Humility is not thinking less of yourself, it's thinking of yourself less.

Birds of a Feather

There's an old saying amongst parrots that 'birds of a feather flock together.' In other words, there's safety in numbers and with the same kind. But you know, that isn't always true. Certainly not in my case....

I've lived with my owner and his family for over 20 years now, and we've built up an extraordinary trust. I'm like an 'honorary' human, and they are like 'honorary' parrots. They all know that I won't harm them, and I know that I'm loved and therefore completely safe. So despite being from different species, we have a unique relationship. There's no fear and no distrust between us. To such an extent that I regularly offer my owner's family a free dental inspection. If my beak can't price any fillings out, they must be in good shape! Of course, my human family could snap their mouths shut on me at any time, but I know they'd never do that.

And then there are the Saturday morning lie-ins. I'm a pretty laid-back bird, so I'll sneak up onto my owner's bed, and join him and his wife for a snooze (lying on my back of course).

Having so much trust and belief in someone is truly very special. And it's rather like the relationship that God and Jesus want to share with us all. Because the more we can trust in God and Jesus, the better equipped we become to deal with the world around us. We develop a greater sense of peace and security, purpose and certainty. A unique bond that can often take many years to develop, and a bond that still needs to be worked on every single day. And there may well be days when things don't go well. There will always be blips along the way. All relationships have to be worked at. But hopefully, over time, the bond and trust will strengthen, and maybe even become rock-solid. And that's the point at which we start to see everything in an entirely new light; both our current world and our place in it, as well as our future in Heaven. And in that future, we begin to see a new kind of order; one in which threat and menace have disappeared, and love and harmony reign. Rather like the vision described in Isaiah, chapter 11:

> The wolf will live with the lamb,
> The leopard will lie down with the goat,
> The calf and the lion and the yearling together;
> And a little child will lead them.
> The cow will feed with the bear,
> Their young will lie down together,
> And the lion will eat straw like the ox ….(Isaiah 11:6–7)

A world without predator and prey; a world of peace and togetherness. A world in which difference is forgotten and unity reigns. My relationships with both God and my human family are just the start of things to come!

Change

Most parrots like to have a regular routine. We like to know what to expect at different times of the day. It gives a pattern to our lives and it helps us to feel more secure. And I'm sure that a great number of humans feel that way too. Especially as they grow older. Because most of us like to hang on to those things that are familiar and 'safe.' I don't really like it when my owner goes on holiday and somebody new has to look after me. Or when I'm supposed to come out for a fly-around at 8.30am, but for whatever reason, it gets shunted back to later in the morning. And then, what about my favourite perches? Over time, they wear out (probably because I've gnawed them!) and they have to be replaced by new ones that simply aren't the same.

The problem for all forms of life here on Earth is that we exist in a state of flux. Nothing stays the same for any length of time. We go from chick (or baby) – to adolescent – to adult – to old age – all in the blink of an eye.

And then there's the seasons which last for little more than three months. I just get myself sorted with all of the right feathers in the right places, and then I have to moult all over again!

And what about relationships? We can form incredibly strong bonds with our loved ones, family members and friends, only to see them move away, or ultimately pass away. Like it or not, we are all existing in a physical world of change.

But does change always have to be a bad thing? Because it certainly keeps us all on our toes. And sometimes change is important for our well-being. Change can bring us closer to God as well as closer to Heaven. In Matthew 18, Jesus tells His squabbling disciples that…

> … unless you change and become like little children, you will never enter the kingdom of Heaven.
>
> (Matthew 18:3)

So Life is all about shaping and moulding us in readiness for Heaven. And we can never change completely by standing still or by clinging on to what we know, like limpets. Because our process of change has to be spiritual rather than physical. The time will come when our physical bodies die and turn to dust. We can't prevent that. But what about our inner part – the 'spiritual core'? Do we think about that enough when we're reaching out for the Botox, the hair dye, and the plastic-surgery brochures? Lives should not be lived out in defiance of change. We're here to evolve in a spiritual sense. A spiritual maturity will bring us closer to God and Jesus. And ultimately, only they can offer us what we really yearn for: *peace, love, stability and a world without change* ....

> Jesus Christ is the same yesterday and today and forever. **(Hebrews 13:8)**

> Therefore, if anyone is in Christ, he is a new creation; the old has gone, the new has come! **(2 Corinthians 5:17)**

In Heaven, there is no such thing as divorce, bereavement, separation, redundancy, financial ruin, illness or death. And there's no worrying about what may or may not be. And there never will be. Heaven is the complete antithesis of all we know and experience here on Earth.

So, as my new lot of feathers start to come through, and irritate and itch, I'm not going to complain. Or when my favourite perch collapses (with me on it), I'll simply shrug my wings. Because in the overall scheme of things, it really doesn't matter. I'll simply focus on what lies ahead – a world of perfection that will never change, and to which we are all invited ....

Christianity, Humour and Fun

All parrots need to have a bit of 'play time.' We like to have things that we can gnaw or preen, things that we can swing on, and things that make a noise. And a small industry has sprung up to supply toys to parrots.

My owner gets a 92 page catalogue through the post which features every kind of 'parrotphernalia.' Bells, rattles, balls, roller-skates – even parrot gymnasiums! And there are some wonderfully named toys such as 'The Holey Roley', 'The Parrot Boing,' 'The Happy Snuggle Tent,' 'The Busy Beak Teaser', 'The Chewtastic', and the 'Parrot Loo Roll.'

I never quite understand why humans go to the trouble of making all these things for parrots when they need to have a lot more fun themselves. You see, humans can be far too serious. They need their downtime just like we do, but so many of them seem to live in a world that's devoid of humour and fun. And sometimes it's because they get 'trapped' within their human systems or by social expectations.

Humans are often told to 'work, work, work' or 'study, study, study' or 'achieve, achieve, achieve!' To spend more hours in the office. To bring in more money for the company. To bring home more money for themselves. To appear 'successful' in worldly terms. And maybe to even become a human celebrity. But at what cost? What are they really doing to themselves and to others in the process?

Wise, old parrots will tell you that over the last 40 years, humans have made their lives far less fun and an awful lot more serious. And over this same period, the recorded rates of human anxiety and depression have absolutely soared. In the developed world, South Korea now has the highest suicide rate amongst its school children. It's also the country that makes its

children study for longer and harder than any other. When the 'serious' side of human life is pushed to its extremes, it can create an opportunity for evil to flourish. There was never any humour or fun under the rule of the Nazis in Germany or the Fascist regimes in Chile and Spain, or the old Communist regimes in East Germany, the Soviet Union and Cambodia. And it's the same today in North Korea or wherever dictatorships hold sway. For when humour and fun disappear, love and compassion go too. And then all of society starts to suffer.

So where do God and Jesus fit into all this? Do they have a sense of humour? Well, you certainly won't find jokes in the Bible, or moments when Jesus let His hair down to become 'one of the lads.' But consider this. God must have a sense of humour and fun to have created parrots! The way we look. The way we talk. The way we walk. Plus our outrageous crests!

At the end of the day, God wants what's best for us all as individuals. He wants us to be in touch with Him, and to live amongst ourselves in peace, love and harmony. And the 'right' sort of fun and humour can go a long way to achieving this. As with everything in life, it's all about finding a sensible balance. There's nothing wrong with working hard, doing your best, or being serious about important things, but we all need some quality downtime, some enjoyment and some fun!

What does a man get for all the toil and anxious striving with which he labours under the sun? All his days his work is pain and grief; even at night his mind does not rest. This too is meaningless. A man can do nothing better than eat and drink and find satisfaction in his work. This too, I see, is from the hand of God .... (Ecclesiastes 2: 22–24)

19

Difference and Diversity

You know, God certainly went to town when He came up with the idea of parrots! We're a really diverse bunch, with some 393 species of us located around the world. And rather like people, we come in all shapes and sizes. We can be small, medium, large or even extra large! We can be both skinny and a bit podgy, ranging from just 12 grams through to 4 kg. And just like humans, we all have our own appearance, character and curious quirks.

I'm sure that you all know how good Amazons and African Greys are at speaking human language. But did you know that there are parrots that can also sing opera? It really is true, and if you want to see it for yourself, simply google 'YouTube opera singing parrots' and then sit back to enjoy the performances! There are also parrots like the Palm Cockatoo that can cause a stir in the neighbourhood by using sticks to drum on hollow tree trunks. There are Military Macaws which fly in splendid formation, rather like a top aerobatics team. And then there's the New Zealand Kea with an unusually shaped beak that's perfectly suited to the scrap-metal business.

Park your car in the wrong place, and it will have been recycled by the time you return. And we mustn't forget the stunning Umbrella Cockatoo, affectionately known in France as the 'Parrotpluie.' (A very useful friend for when it's raining).

Yes, parrots could teach you humans a thing or two about diversity. Although there are so many different types of parrot with so many individual traits, on the whole, we all get on with one another. Diversity gives the parrot family a unique richness, and it should be just the same for humans as well. After all, we've all been crafted by the same Creator.

In the Bible, the promise of Salvation is there for everyone, irrespective of their nationality, ethnicity and cultural background. You see, difference doesn't have to be seen as a threat. In fact, quite the opposite. We've all been given unique gifts and talents and it's important that we share these in a positive way. So that everyone benefits and we all become enriched!

For there is no difference between Jew and Gentile – the same Lord is Lord of all and richly blesses all who call on him, for everyone who calls on the name of the Lord will be saved.   (Romans 10:12–13)

Accept one another, then, just as Christ accepted you .... 　　　　　　　　　　　　　　 (Romans 15:7a)

Make every effort to live in peace with all men .... 　　　　　　　　　　　　　　　　 (Hebrews 12:14a)

Do I Really Matter?

Even by parrot standards, I'm really rather small. Approximately nine inches from head to tail. And when I think of myself as one small bird on the face of this planet, then I can feel terribly small. Rather like an insignificant ant or a fly or even a speck of dust. And for some humans, as well as parrots, life events can squash us down into believing this. We ask questions such as: 'What am I doing here?' 'Would anyone notice if I wasn't here anymore?' 'Does my existence really matter?' And then there's that old chestnut which always seems to come around: 'What is the purpose of my existence? Am I simply a statistic?'

Lots of us struggle to find a real identity and sense of purpose in life. And some of us can become the butt of cruel jokes. I was once asked what you get when you cross a parrot with a centipede. The answer was a 'walkie talkie.' I was mortified!

But you know, it's when things are stacked against us, or when we feel insignificant, that God loves us the most. He's not so interested in big egos or power-complexes, or with those that shout loudest so that others come running to them. No, God, through Jesus here on Earth, placed a great emphasis upon the

poor, the humble, the lowly and the suffering. Those 'insignificant specks of dust' that society can so easily ignore and trample upon. Beggars, rough sleepers, the disabled, the paralysed, the dying and even the ladies of the night. Humans that were alive, but in some cases, only just.

And so, when Jesus chose His first disciples, He didn't look in the direction of the rich or famous, the powerful or the celebrities of His day. No, He decided to recruit a bunch of humble fishermen. Simon, James and John. Men who probably hadn't received a proper education, and who were existing pretty much at subsistence level. If they caught fish, they ate. If they didn't, they went hungry.

Jesus chose them ahead of everybody else. And by doing this, and by spending so much time with the poor and the lowly, Jesus was telling the world that 'we all matter.' We all matter very much! We can be insignificant in human terms, but it's not human terms that count. It's not about our health, our strength, our intelligence, our worldliness, our wealth or our social standing. And neither is it about our past transgressions. Because we will always be cherished and valued by our Creator. We are all God's invention, His creation and His unique beings. So never feel small, alone or forgotten. God loves us and cares for us, warts and all, whoever and wherever we may be.

Are not five sparrows sold for two pennies? Yet not one of them is forgotten by God. Indeed, the very hairs of your head are all numbered. Don't be afraid; you are worth more than many sparrows.   Luke 12:6–7

Easter in Lockdown

Despite the current suffering of the world around, I've felt an inner joy throughout the Easter weekend. It's not that I've shut out the painful cries of humanity. I still care very deeply. But I've continued to walk with a swagger and a strut. And I still do my daily exercise routine on the kitchen clothes airer. Because in all of the current darkness, I sense a great light....

We've all experienced a very strange Holy Week. Normally, millions of humans around the world would have been flocking into their local churches to pay witness to the crucifixion and resurrection of Jesus Christ. And yet those heavy old church doors have remained locked and bolted throughout. Instead, humans have been largely confined to their homes. In many cases, people have just spent Easter separated from their loved ones and special friends, or maybe grieving for those who have been taken by the virus.

The church is normally the very place to which folk turn in a time of crisis. But the current lockdown means we find ourselves in a strange kind of limbo, rather as the world must have felt on that original Easter Saturday, caught between Jesus' death and resurrection. But I hope that's not a place in which we're stuck. Because Easter doesn't just belong to one specific time of the year. We should be living and breathing the significance of Easter *every* day of our lives. And although those church doors may be firmly shut, during this crisis, we're being given an extraordinary opportunity to unlock and unbolt our hearts and souls to let God and Jesus enter in....

For now, 'the church' has to be inside each one of us. Because God and Jesus can exist inside us wherever we happen to be. On Good Friday, on Easter Day, and on any other day of the year. In our thoughts, our actions, our energy and our prayers.

And that's what appears to be happening right now in so many different places. Humans, many of whom don't usually 'do' religion, are beginning to turn to God and Jesus in prayer. Prayers are being said for individuals and loved ones; for the amazing army of selfless medics and care workers; for the sick and the grieving; for the frightened and the lost. Even our politicians are referring to prayer. Many hearts and souls are being laid bare to God and Jesus for the very first time. So many humans are looking out for their loved ones and neighbours and friends in a way that would have seemed impossible only a few weeks ago. Our churches may have been closed for Easter, but the spirit of God and Jesus has rarely been more alive amongst the people of the world.

This has been a very different Eastertime. An Easter that's taken on a whole new meaning and relevance for so many humans beings. Because the sacrifice and resurrection of Jesus Christ and His gift of Salvation have become very real. A shining light in the midst of so much darkness and despair. The extraordinary, mind-boggling gift of deliverance from all of the troubles of this world. That is the essence of Easter joy. And certainly cause for a strut and a swagger and a clothes airer workout!

For God did not send his Son into the world to condemn the world, but to save the world through him.
(John 3:17)

Feeling Welcome

If a new human visits our house, and I feel comfortable with them, I usually lift and then open my wings. It's a kind of warm parrot welcome which is intended to say that 'I like you and trust you.'

The world is full of 'strangers' who want to feel both welcome and wanted. And in parts of the Czech Republic, many humans still practise the particularly nice custom of laying an extra place at the family dinner table, just in case someone should turn up at the door.

And it can be quite daunting when we enter a place without knowing anyone else there. Such as the day I first came home with my human owner. A first day at school or university. Starting a new job. Or walking into a church for the very first time. In all of these situations, a genuine, warm welcome is something very precious.

Welcoming strangers is a part of Christian love. It breaks down division and barriers of distrust. It achieves unity and common ground. When the radio is on, I often hear about the troubles between the Israelis and the Palestinians. Wouldn't it be wonderful if somehow, they could reach out to one another, shake hands, invite one another into their homes – and build bridges instead of walls.

Jesus reminds us that when we make the effort to welcome someone – whoever it may be – we are in fact welcoming Him into our lives ....

And whoever welcomes a little child like this in My name welcomes Me. (Matthew 18:5).

Over the next few days, many of us will have an opportunity to make someone feel welcome. They may not be like us. They may be quite different. But difference and diversity are all a part of God's creation. And ultimately, warmth and love can bring us all together.

There is neither Jew nor Greek, slave nor free, male nor female, for you are all one in Christ Jesus. (Galatians 3:28)

Finding Your Right Environment

It's true to say, that along with many other birds, parrots have extremely large feet. In fact, compared to our body size, our feet probably equate to size 30+ in the human world. That's why when we walk, we have a swagger, (a bit like John Wayne in his cowboy outfit).

You humans probably find this very comical, but I'd like to see you hang on to a branch in the top of a tree with the feet and toes that you've been given. You see, our toes aren't so good on the ground, but they're brilliant for wrapping around branches. And there's a bit of wisdom here for us all to consider. Because it's all too easy to dismiss or laugh at someone when you see them struggling along. But place them in a different environment, and a totally different person (or parrot) can emerge. Suddenly, they come into their own. For example, a frustrated bricklayer could turn out to be a brilliant artist, given the right surroundings in which to flourish. Or a taxi driver could turn out to be the Prime Minister or President that their country has been crying out for.

And then there's the whole issue of a Christian environment. How many people around the world would have discovered God and the Christian faith if they had only found themselves in a different environment? If they hadn't been subject to the push-pull effect of so many other forces and influences? Maybe their families simply 'didn't do church' when they were growing up. Or, maybe in adult life, the worldly allure of wealth, power and success led them along a different path. There are a million different influences out there which can keep us apart from the Christian message. The same Christian message that can secure our future place in Heaven – surely our ultimate environment.

Christianity should never be forced upon anyone. It needs to be discovered. But all of us that have a deep inner faith should be making a statement to the world. Through the way that we live and the things that we say. Through what we choose to do or to avoid. And through the light that we shine out around us. Because that light comes from God, and He can use every one of us to spread His presence in the world.

You are the light of the world. A city on a hill cannot be hidden. Neither do people light a lamp and put it under a bowl. Instead they put it on its stand, and it gives light to everybody in the house. In the same way, let your light shine before men, that they may see your good deeds and praise your Father in Heaven.
(Matthew 5:14–16)

For Those Who Suffer

My owner had a surprise the other day. He went to use the mop and bucket in the kitchen, and there in the bottom of the bucket, nestling up to the mop head, was a small bat. And a very comatose bat at that. It was in a state of semi-hibernation, hidden away from the rain and the cold and everything else that bats don't like.

There are probably a lot of humans right now that would feel envious of that bat. The nights are getting longer; the days are getting colder. And Covid 19 is becoming more prevalent, resulting in another national lockdown. The mood across the nation is very flat, and so many humans are feeling very worried. Worried about loneliness, depression and isolation. Worried about their jobs and finances and livelihoods. Worried about being unable to visit their loved ones. And simply worried about how they are going to cope and survive. This is a really challenging time to be a human being.

Parrots don't worry in quite the same way as humans. Because we live our lives one day at a time. We focus on the here and now and not on what tomorrow may bring. Simply being alive to enjoy another day is a triumph in itself, and so we try to make the most of each and every day. It's just like Jesus said to the crowds:

> Therefore I tell you, do not worry about your life, what you will eat or drink; or about your body, what you will wear. Is not life more important than food, and the body more important than clothes? Look at the birds of the air; they do not sow or reap or store away in barns, and yet your heavenly Father feeds them ....
> (Matthew 6:25–26a)

The more complex humans make their world, the more they have to worry about. And too much complexity blocks out the view. Sometimes we need to see through the crisis to what awaits us on the other side ....

> I consider that our present sufferings are not worth comparing with the glory that will be revealed ....
> (Romans 8:18).

There may be times when we need to experience hardship to allow us to see the light. There's an old parrot saying which goes:

> *'When you find yourself in a dark place, you may think you've been buried, when actually, you've been planted.'*

We should always have hope during our darkest days because we were created by a force of love and compassion. And the real challenge is for us to see that and understand it. And to realise that there is far more to our existence than the immediate threats that lurk around us.

If you look at the world, you'll be distressed. If you look within, you'll be depressed. But if you look at Christ, you'll be at rest.
(Corrie ten Boon: 1892–1983. *Dutch author and concentration camp survivor*).

Love and Grief

Every living creature here on Earth will experience both life and death. It's all part of a kind of 'predetermined package'. And the more sophisticated creatures such as humans and parrots will also experience the emotion of grief when a loved one dies. My owner's recently been grieving after the passing of a special friend. He has absolutely no doubt that his friend is now in Heaven, free from all pain and discomfort, and yet he still grieves. Why should that be? Is he being selfish? Or is his faith not as strong as he makes out?

There's a kind of irony in the relationship between grief and love. Because as Christians, we are expected to love one another. Love forms the very essence of God, Jesus and the Holy Spirit. But the more love we carry inside ourselves, the more we are leaving ourselves open to the emotion of grief. The two go hand in hand. And grief is indiscriminate. It affects everyone irrespective of whether they have a Christian faith or not. Just as William Shakespeare once said:

> Every one can master grief but he that has it.
> **(William Shakespeare)**

Jesus knew all about the emotion of grief. When Lazarus has apparently died, and his sister Mary is in the grip of grief, Jesus Himself wells up:

> When Jesus saw her weeping, and the Jews who
> had come along with her also weeping, he was
> deeply moved in spirit and troubled ... Jesus wept ...
> **(John 11:33–35)**

Grief is the price that all of us on Earth must pay for the blessing of love. Even that old favourite amongst parrots – Winnie The Pooh – realised this as he was saying his final farewells to Christopher Robin in the Enchanted Forest …

How lucky I am to have something that makes saying goodbye so hard. (*Winnie The Pooh*: A.A. Milne)

Prior to this, Christopher Robin reminds us all that we can surprise ourselves by the way we handle separation and grief:

If ever there is a tomorrow when we're not together, there is something you must always remember: you are braver than you believe, stronger than you seem, and smarter than you think. But the most important thing is even if we're apart … I'll always be with you. (*Christopher Robin*: A.A. Milne)

People we love help to mould and to shape us. They leave a lasting impression, and they leave us with memories. And for Christians, these memories help to bridge the gap until we are once more reunited with those that we miss.

Now is your time of grief, but I will see you again and you will rejoice, and no-one will take away your joy. (John 16:22)

Blessed are those who mourn for they will be comforted. (Matthew 5:4)

Do not let your hearts be troubled. Trust in God; trust also in me. In my Father's house are many rooms … I am going there to prepare a place for you. (John 14:1–2)

Getting Your Reward in Heaven

I guess there's a little part in everyone of us that wants to be appreciated. We want to be acknowledged for small acts of kindness, for our efforts and for our sincerity. And when nothing is said, or we get the opposite reaction to the one we were hoping for, it can leave us feeling hurt or disappointed.

And that applies to parrots as well as to human beings. For example, I can go a whole day without gnawing the top of the kitchen cabinets, but does anyone notice? No, instead they complain that I've spilt seed husks all over the floor. Or when I whistle a special tune that I've worked on for ages, instead of stopping to listen, the family rushes out of the door to go shopping. Life isn't always very fair. But when I'm having a bad day, I think about a special message that Mother Teresa of Calcutta had pinned up on her wall. This is what it says:

People are often unreasonable, irrational and self-centred. Forgive them anyway.

If you are kind, people may accuse you of selfish, ulterior motives. Be kind anyway.

If you are successful, you will win some unfaithful friends and some genuine enemies. Succeed anyway.

If you are honest and sincere, people may deceive you. Be honest and sincere anyway.

What you spend time creating others could destroy overnight. Create anyway.

If you find serenity and happiness, some may be jealous. Be happy anyway.

The good you do today will often be forgotten. Do good anyway.

Give the best you have, and it will never be enough. Give your best anyway.

So, whether you're having a bad day or not, ...

In the final analysis, it is between you and God. It has never been between you and them anyway ... .

(Mother Teresa of Calcutta: 1910–1997. *Posthumously made a Saint by the Catholic Church for her missionary work in Calcutta, India)*

Rejoice and be glad, because great is your reward in heaven ... . (Matthew 5:12a).

Gifts for Christmas

Christmas shopping for parrots is a lot easier than it is for humans. We might pick a succulent morsel out of our food pots and offer it to a loved one, or we might offer to preen somebody's tail for them. But that's as far as it goes. We don't need to worry about spending money or doing the wrapping up.

In the human world, Christmas shopping is now in full swing. And it can be very difficult for humans to know what to buy everyone. Those Three Wise Men have a lot to answer for in starting the whole tradition of Christmas gifts. If they hadn't rolled into Bethlehem with their gold, myrrh and frankincense, then humans might not have come up with the idea of Christmas presents at all!

But you know, even if the baby Jesus isn't physically in front of us this Christmas, there's nothing to stop us from giving Him a Christmas present, if we really want to. And this is where Christina Rossetti's classic Christmas carol 'In The Bleak Mid-Winter' comes to mind. Verse four goes like this:

What can I give Him,
Poor as I am?
If I were a shepherd,
I would bring a lamb;
If I were a wise man,
I would do my part;
Yet what I can I give Him –
Give my heart.

The greatest gift we can give to Jesus – or to fellow parrots, or to human beings – is our heart. In other words, pure, genuine, all-encompassing love.

A few Christmases ago, I heard about a local human family – a young husband, wife and their two children – who placed all of their Christmas present funds into a joint kitty. Then they went together to their local supermarket, and spent all of the money on a range of Christmas food and treats. But none of it was for them. They took everything they'd bought to the local foodbank in Barnstaple. So they all went without their own Christmas gifts, to help others less fortunate than themselves. And this wasn't simply a gift to the foodbank or to all of the people that it helped. No, this was the most beautiful gift for Jesus (whether they realised it or not). Far greater than the gold, myrrh and frankincense delivered to Jesus by the Three Wise Men. And even to this day, this small, unknown family from Barnstaple probably aren't aware of the full impact of their gift.

So as we think about our Christmas shopping, let's not forget about those gifts which Jesus would really like us to offer. The gift of our heart. The gift of ourselves. And the gift of going without something ourselves, so that others may be helped and cared for.

Each one must give as he has decided in his heart, not reluctantly or under compulsion, for God loves a cheerful giver. **(2 Corinthians 9:7)**

Giving Back

I'd been gnawing my perch all morning, and creating a pile of sawdust on the floor, when I suddenly decided that this shouldn't be the way I live my life. Because there's a balance to be made between taking (or in my case, destroying) the gifts of life for our own enjoyment, and giving something back to others. And I recalled how Albert Einstein had once said:

> It is every man's obligation to put back into the world at least the equivalent of what he takes out of it.
>
> (Albert Einstein: 1879–1955.
> *German-born physicist*)

So maybe I should start planting some trees around my cage ....

The problem is that for so many of us, the more we get, the more we want, and then the more we think only of ourselves. It's always been this way, and it's why Jesus once commented:

> How hard it is for the rich to enter the kingdom of God! Indeed, it is easier for a camel to go through the eye of a needle than for a rich man to enter the kingdom of God.
>
> (Luke 18:24b–25)

So it's always a breath of fresh air to hear about someone that decides to give something back to the world. One such human was Andrew Carnegie. After humble beginnings in Scotland, he moved with his family to America where he earned a fortune from the U.S. steel industry. By 1901, he was worth $480 million, but he eventually gave some $350 million of this to charitable causes. His philosophy was that: *'A man who dies rich dies disgraced.'*

But of course, you don't have to be rich to be able to give back to society. The world is now going through a time of great crisis as the Coronavirus spreads into every different society. If ever there was a time for sharing and giving back, this is it. And that not only applies to the Andrew Carnegies of this world, but to all of us. By giving and sharing whatever we can, irrespective of how rich or poor or frail or strong we happen to be. Think of what that splendid human Captain Sir Tom Moore was able to achieve during the final year of his life. Collectively we can all make a huge impact on the suffering of the world around us – and that applies to both the human and natural worlds. If we possess any amount of wealth at all, or the determination of Captain Sir Tom Moore, then we have the power in our hands. The question is what we choose to do with it ....

If you're in the luckiest 1% of humanity, you owe it to the rest of humanity to think about the other 99%.
(Warren Buffet: 1930–present. *American business tycoon*).

As He looked up, Jesus saw the rich putting their gifts into the temple treasury. He also saw a poor widow put in two very small copper coins. 'I tell you the truth,' He said, 'this poor widow has put in more than all of the others'. (Luke 21:1–3)

God's Personal Message for Us Today

We parrots are masters of communication! We express ourselves in so many different ways. Our vocal range can cover everything from contented purrs to raucous squawks. Or wolf-whistles through to police car sirens. Or kissing noises through to the theme tunes of favourite T.V. shows. And the more clever birds amongst us know when to make the right sound at the right time. For example, when my owner's wife returns home from work, I'll make the sound of a welcome kiss before my owner gets anywhere near her.

Of course, human communication is far more complicated. Apart from normal speech, you have phone messages, texts, faxes, Facebook, WhatsApp. and all sorts of other technical wizardry. In fact, scientists say that humans spend around 70–80% of their day engaged in some form of communication. But with so much communication flying around, I wonder whether you manage to sift out the messages that really matter?

So what do you look at? What do you ignore? What do you respond to? What do you forget? What's relevant, and what's wasting your time? And I'm asking these questions for a very important reason. Because God tries to communicate with us every single day. A unique, personal message, with our name on it. For example, when you were walking down the street earlier in the day, and you passed a rough-looking down-and-out holding up a cardboard sign in your direction: did it really have anything to do with you? The sign read: 'Seeking Human Kindness.'

And what about all of those other messages in your 'In-Box' that you haven't yet read? The ones that say: 'Your sins are forgiven'; 'I have a plan for you;' 'I haven't forgotten you during this difficult time;' 'Pray to me, and then we can talk.' Do you bother reading these, or do you just consign them to your 'Trash' folder? We receive these messages in all kinds of different ways. Sometimes we get a deep 'spiritual knowing.' Sometimes it will come from an off-

the-cuff comment made by a friend. Or we might find ourselves stripped bare in the midst of a crisis which has left us more open to seeking 'the unthinkable.' Or sometimes, an extraordinary coincidence comes along that is far more than just a coincidence….

Every single message will be as unique as we are. And all that we are asked to do is take the time to listen or to read, and then process. That's all there is to it.

Few of us are brilliant at listening. But the key to life is this. For us to listen to and act upon enough of God's messages so that we're shaped and formed into something new, fulfilling our potential as a part of God's creation….

Don't you know that you yourselves are God's temple and that God's spirit lives in you? (1 Corinthians: 3:16)

For it is God who works inside you to make you willing to act according to his good purpose.

(Philippians 2:13. *Amended slightly for better flow*.)

God Within Us

Last week, I was sitting on my perch listening to that human cockatoo called 'Boris' as he was warning humans about a 'bumpy ride' ahead. With Covid cases rising and a cold dark Winter looming, I feel rather sorry for humans right now.

Of course, some humans will view these challenges in a positive way. Back in the 1920's and 30's, at the time of the Great Depression in America, Henry Ford said this:

When everything seems to be going against you, remember that the airplane takes off against the wind, and not with it.

(Henry Ford: 1863–1947.
Founder of the Ford Motor Company).

But there will also be a great many humans questioning where the presence of God is right now, as they do whenever tragedy strikes or hard times prevail. So if there really is a God, why doesn't He get rid of the coronavirus for the sake of the world? Why hasn't He done so already? So many people are losing loved ones, their jobs, their savings, their freedom and their sanity ....

But when we ask questions like that, we are in a sense, denying our own responsibility for helping the world. Because everyone has a part to play, but we don't always see it. Instead it's easier to blame others for any misfortune, especially politicians and God.

There's no doubt that God, as creator of our world, could instantly step in to halt the coronavirus, and bring peace and harmony to the human world. But that's not how He chooses to operate. Not since Jesus left the Earth. Instead God mainly works through all of us collectively. From deep within each individual. From inside anyone that invites Him in; through humans that live out their lives with an abundance of love, compassion, justice and goodness in their hearts. The very qualities that make folk want to give, to help, to care and to share. And so every time humans turn away from these things, they are in effect turning away from God and cutting Him out of the world in which they live.

We've all been created and designed to bring the presence of God into our world through our thoughts, our words and our actions. Through our work, our voice, our compassion, our gifts, our listening, our hope and our very presence. It's only by living with the presence of God in our hearts that we can overcome Life's huge challenges.

Hopefully the pandemic will bring all humans closer together in a good way. The same kind of silver lining to those dark clouds that Henry Ford saw all those years ago. But ultimately, it all comes down to us. How we choose to react. What we choose to hold dear in our hearts. And what we give out to the world around us ....

> Don't you know that you yourselves are God's temple and that God's Spirit lives in you? (1 Corinthians 3:16)
>
> I pray that ... He may strengthen you with power through his Spirit in your inner being, so that Christ may dwell in your hearts ... .
> (Ephesians 3:16–17a)

Growing the Seed of Life

My owner's been a very busy fellow, working out in the garden, and sowing all kinds of seeds. He's trying to grow lots of vegetables in case there's a shortage during the coronavirus lockdown.

But you know, you don't have to go out and buy a packet of seeds in order to grow something good. For as that great hymn writer Charles Wesley once said, 'God's grace is like a seed planted inside us all.' Each of us carries that tiny seed within our make-up. And in a great many of us, it will eventually start to grow.

And we parrots are extremely perceptive. There have been lots of times when I've sensed God's presence shining out of humans in front of me. Through their eyes, their smile and their whole demeanour. They have an aura of God about them because they are filled by God's presence. Deep inside them, the seed of God's grace has not only germinated, but also started to grow and to flourish.

During the current coronavirus lockdown, so many humans have asked the question: 'Where is God in all this?' And part of the answer is that He's actually inside a great many of us. Even when we don't realise it. Otherwise, why would we want to care for the sick and the elderly? Why go shopping for our neighbour? Why did we volunteer to take a friend to a hospital appointment when we could have been sitting outside in the sunshine?

Part of the process of coming to faith is realising where our inner force of 'goodness' comes from. And yes, it's all wrapped up within that miniscule seed planted deep within us. And the more we allow it to grow and to flourish, the more we can do for God in this world. And the more we begin to understand. C.S. Lewis once said:

I believe in Christianity as I believe that the sun has risen: not only because I see it, but because by it I see everything else.
(C.S. Lewis: 1898–1963. *Writer and lay theologian*)

It's this realisation and new perception which sets Christian people apart from others. It's what led the evangelist, Billy Graham to once say:

My home is in Heaven. I'm just travelling through the world.
(Billy Graham: 1918–2018. *American evangelist*)

Of course, none of us will ever be perfect. But the more we allow ourselves to become filled by God's Spirit, the more work we will do as God's envoys here on Earth. And hopefully, we will play some small part in making this world a better place for all ....

But the fruit of the Spirit is love, joy, peace, patience, kindness, goodness, faithfulness, gentleness and self-control.
(Galatians 5:22–23a)

Happy New Year! (?)

Hello everyone! A Very Happy New Year to you all, even if it doesn't seem like a happy one right now. Brexit issues, covid, lockdowns, work and financial worries – for many humans, this is proving to be a very challenging time.

But even in the good times, the beginning of a New Year can seem very bittersweet. It's a time when many humans pause to take stock of their lives and situations, and so often, there's something missing. New Year parties and the good life can offer a quick and temporary fix, but they only paper over an emptiness beneath. And it's this same feeling of emptiness which is captured in the opening lyrics of the Abba song, 'Happy New Year:'

'No more champagne
And the fireworks are through
Here we are, me and you
Feeling lost and feeling blue.
It's the end of the party
And the morning seems so
grey ….'

And then comes the familiar chorus, 'Happy New Year,' and a rather desperate vision of a world in which *'every neighbour is a friend.'*

The song is a striking paradox. It's got an outwardly catchy, upbeat chorus which glosses over the empty void described in the lyrics. And how true that is right now for so many folk around the world. There's a gaping hole within the jigsaw puzzle of so many human lives. And so often, we make New Year's resolutions

in an attempt to fill that hole. Some humans believe that losing weight or taking out a gym membership provides the instant fix. For others, it might be finding that special person to share their lives with, getting a new job, or aiming for promotion and a bigger salary. And some of these things will certainly help, but none of them will make a person's life puzzle complete. Because ultimately, there's only one special piece that will fit, and that's the love and presence of Jesus Christ.

When Jesus spoke again to the people, he said: 'I am the light of the world. Whoever follows me will never walk in darkness, but will have the light of life.
(John: 8:12)

All of that inner restlessness and striving – that sense of dissatisfaction and emptiness – none of this can ever be fully laid to rest by what our current world has to offer. Only a spiritual fulfilment can achieve that. A life lived with the presence of Jesus. So that we discover a real purpose, a reason and above all – hope – for our lives. Special gifts that will sustain us through the good times and the bad.

So I say again: 'Happy New Year everyone!' Who knows what this New Year has in store? But we can get through it all, come what may, by living our lives with Jesus!

Helping Others

Well, it's nearly Christmas time now. Just one week to go. And Christmas is a time when parrots can have great fun around the house. I can really let my crest down and do exciting things like climbing up the Christmas Tree or swinging upside-down on the strings of Christmas lights. And when no one's looking, I can go and eat all of the berries off the holly that the humans have hung up in the hallway. Happy days! But of course, Christmas isn't always such a happy time for everybody. In fact, for many, it can be a very difficult time. And somehow, at Christmas time, the needs of the world become more etched within our inner conscience. They rattle around and nag us more than at any other time of the year. The plight of the world's sick, the elderly, the lonely and the bereaved.

The hungry, the poor, and the homeless. Maybe, subconsciously, we're aware that God is about to give us the most precious gift of all in the form of Jesus, so that we want to give something back. And that's where as Christians, we can all rally 'round. By thinking of others and helping where we can. By giving up some of our time, or by giving financially. A great many humans will give more to charity in the run-up to Christmas than at any other time of the year.

We all have the ability to do something to help others in need around us. As for me, I took pity on the garden Robin who was shivering outside my window. I invited him in to sit on my perch and warm himself up. One tiny act, but something that made a real difference. Multiply that a thousand times, and just think what could be achieved. Which is why the Bible has so much to say on this subject:

Each of you should look not only to your own interests, but also to the interests of others.   (Philippians 2:4)

Therefore, as we have the opportunity, let us do good to all people … .
(Galatians 6:10a)

Carry each other's burdens, and in this way you will fulfil the law of Christ
(Galatians 6:2)

So Happy Christmas everyone. And let's make it a Happy Christmas for the world around us!

Humility and Pollywood

I'm sure that you're all very familiar with Hollywood in California, and Bollywood in India. Some of you may also have heard of Nollywood – the hub of the African film-making industry based in Nigeria. But have you ever come across 'Pollywood'?

Pollywood is where you go if you're a parrot that's 'made it big' in life. Parrot business tycoons like Quill Gates, parrot popstars like The Beaky Boys, and parrot sports stars such as David Peck'em (yes, he always was a bit of a dirty player) – they all flock to Pollywood to announce to the world that 'they've arrived'.

Successful parrots go there to strut and to swagger and to head-bang their way up and down the red carpet, while all of their adoring fans look on. A thriving industry has sprung up around them there including parrot petting parlours, feather spas and high-end crest coiffeurs. It's a totally different world.

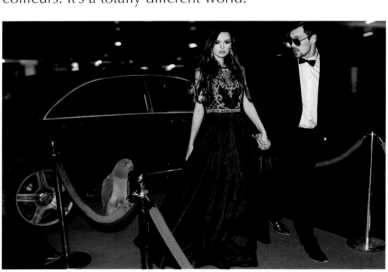

Thanks to my weekly blogs and this book, I've become quite famous, so I received an invitation to attend a function in Pollywood. But do you know what?

I turned it down. Because flaunting my fame and success wouldn't make me a better parrot. I don't fancy living in an artificial world which can initially lift you high up into the air, but then leave you to crash back to Earth later on.

To be true Christians – to keep in touch with God – we need to keep humility within our hearts. The nicest humans and parrots that I've met in my life have always carried a nugget of humility in their make-up. Humility is at the core of the Christian faith. Jesus was born inside a lowly stable and not in some glitzy palace. He lived in poverty when He had the power to make Himself very rich or walk upon a red carpet. And the Gospels place a huge emphasis upon the poor, the needy and the downtrodden, while the wealthy and successful people of Jesus' era rarely get a positive mention. The book of Proverbs (11.2) tells us that '... with humility comes wisdom.' And 1 Peter gives us this very emphatic instruction:

> All of you, clothe yourselves with humility towards one another, because God opposes the proud, but gives grace to the humble. (1Peter: 5:5b)

Heaven is a level playing field. It doesn't matter if you're a down-and-out, a huge rock star, a toilet cleaner, or the President of the United States. A nugget of humility within your hearts provides the fuel for your journey along the highway into Heaven.

I Don't Do Christianity

I was recently having a good preen on my perch and listening to humans talking on the radio. And not for the first time, I heard somebody say: 'I don't do Christianity or religion.' And I thought to myself how wrong you are. Because most of us in the western world do 'do' Christianity, whether we're aware of it or not. Because the teachings of Jesus form the bedrock of the modern western societies in which we exist. Jesus gave us all a model for good living here on Earth, and although there will always be room for improvement, most western societies largely keep to His teachings. And it's not simply a case of abiding by the Ten Commandments – murder, stealing, adultery and all the rest . . . .

Jesus offered us a new vision for living; a set of ideals that were totally revolutionary for their time. His teaching was that we should all value everybody equally. Irrespective of status, age, power, culture, race, wealth and gender (Galatians 3:28). And the parable of The Good Samaritan adds compassion into the mix (Luke 10:25–37). The same compassion that we see today in the work of the wonderful NHS, Social Security systems, and the care of vulnerable humans in society. Race, ethnicity and cultural background don't come into the equation.

Jesus also taught humans to respect and pay their dues to the government of

the day (Luke 20:25b), to value humility above almost everything else, and to pursue peace and love in all walks of life.

The worst examples of human suffering have usually occurred when Jesus' formula for living has been replaced by secular human ideals. Just think about the rise of the Nazi party in Germany, or Stalinism in the U.S.S.R.

The story of Jesus isn't simply some old fairy tale belonging to the distant past. Jesus was the Son of God who came to Earth to

change humanity for the better and to offer everyone the hope of eternal life. And He's still very much present in our modern society, more than 2000 years on. He achieved His legacy without wealth or possessions; without political influence or an army; without violence or worldly power or a proper education. This same Jesus who could convey more wisdom and meaning in a single sentence than 1000 scholars could achieve in a wordy doctrine. The wisdom, the power and the influence of Jesus knows no boundary in space or time. So we all 'do' Christianity to some extent, whether we know it or not.

Blessed are the poor in spirit, for theirs is the kingdom of God.
Blessed are those who mourn for they will be comforted.
Blessed are the meek, for they will inherit the earth.
Blessed are those who hunger and thirst for righteousness for they will be filled.
Blessed are the merciful for they will be shown mercy.
Blessed are the pure in heart for they will see God.
Blessed are the peacemakers, for they will be called Sons of God.
Blessed are those who are persecuted because of righteousness for theirs is the kingdom of Heaven.   (Matthew 5:3–10)

If the Weight of the World Seems Too Great

I wonder if you're a bit like me when you wake up in the morning? I wake up as the first light of day delicately creeps in through the kitchen window. I cautiously open one eye and peer out from under my wing, wondering what the new day will deliver. And sometimes, I don't really want to wake up and face the world at all. Because when I went to sleep the previous night, I knew that Covid 19 was continuing to ravage the world. That the humans in Beirut were still in desperate need after last week's mega explosion. That lots of other humans are jobless and homeless. That millions of innocent humans are continuing to suffer in the Yemen, in shanty towns and refugee camps. And that some of my nearest and dearest are going through very tough times....

The enormity of human suffering can seem overwhelming. Too much for us to deal with when we wake up in the morning. It's far easier to simply shut it all out, and to focus on ourselves. After all, none of us can carry the weight of the world on our shoulders; not even if you've got broad wings like me.

And yet, as Christians, we're asked not to ignore the needs of others, but to embrace them through love, compassion, empathy and generosity. Hang on a minute! I'm only a small parrot. How on earth can I do all that? Well, here's how it works....

Those of us who are able, can give to charity. Others can give of themselves, spending time or working with others less fortunate. And the rest of us can simply pray. We can lift up to God the entire suffering of the world.

And by doing so, we're admitting that we can't exist without Him. Our long-term happiness depends upon both God and Jesus.

Recognising the needs of the world, feeling compassion and empathising with others – all of this pushes us closer to God. Because it's putting God at the centre of human suffering where He is most needed. Through praying, we are encouraging God's spirit to flow down onto the raging fires of human existence, dampening them down with His balm of love, comfort, strength and hope. So that all of us are better able to deal with adversity. And so that we're reminded that another world awaits us; one that is free of fire, suffering and distress ....

> Now the dwelling of God is with men .... He will wipe every tear from their eyes. There will be no more death or mourning or crying or pain, for the old order of things has passed away.　　　　(Revelation: 21:3b–4)

So, after a tentative start, I've now woken up today feeling good! I'm strutting my stuff up and down my perch. Because I know that come what may, I'll never be alone. The suffering of the world will never crush me so long as I ask God to help bear the weight, both for myself and for those for whom I pray every day ....

Imperfect Perfection

I have a flaw in my character which I share with nearly all other parrots. Because I am totally vain. I spend every spare minute preening my feathers to perfection. Because like most other parrots, I want to be the best looking bird in town. So every feather has to be perfectly in place and displayed to maximum effect. It's all about achieving an instant visual impact. So that others judge and value me according to what they see at first glance. And our feathers often serve as a rather shallow disguise because we're not always as perfect on the inside as we would have others believe.

It's a flaw that's all too common in the human world as well. So many humans create an image of themselves on social media to give the impression that they are beautiful people 'living out the dream.' But so often it's all a sad deception. Because anyone pretending to be something that they're not, can't be very happy

at the core. They have to create an illusion because they don't like what they see, or else they're afraid of being judged by others. And this is no way to live out a life. Some might call it tragic or dishonest. But for millions of humans around the world, this is all part of a daily routine.

And not even the church escapes. Vicars and Readers often wear those traditional white gowns and vestments which are intended to give an impression of purity. And yet we know that no humans, or other living creatures, will ever be totally pure. We're all ultimately sinners whether we like that label or not. So why the pretence?

It wouldn't be such a bad thing if somebody 'accidentally' spilt a cup of coffee all over us. Because the brown stains would help to visualize the sinful 'smudges' that we hide away inside. A few 'stains' and 'smudges' on the outside would make us true to ourselves, and honest before God. The book of 1 Samuel reminds us that:

> The Lord does not look at the things that man looks at. Man looks at the outward appearance, but the Lord looks at the heart. **(1 Samuel: 16:7b)**.

Deep down, I believe that much of creation wants to be loved and accepted, and to offer love back. But so often, this 'love' becomes confused with 'self-image.' And we forget that love '…does not envy, it does not boast…' and '…it is not proud.' (1 Corinthians 13: 4b).

So, maybe I should give up on the preening today. Which probably means having an adventure deep inside the kitchen bin, and coming out later, well and truly 'smudged.' Because then I'm hiding nothing and I'm being true to myself!

YOU DON'T HAVE TO BE PERFECT TO BE AMAZING

The Pharisee stood up and prayed about himself: 'God, I thank you that I am not like other men – robbers, evildoers, adulterers – or even like this tax collector ….' But the tax collector stood at a distance. He would not even look up to Heaven, but beat his breast and said, 'God, have mercy on me, a sinner.' (Luke 18:11–13)

Is a Feather Simply a Feather?

Is a feather simply a feather? Or is it really a work of art? Are all feathers the same? Or are they all unique?

Being a Senegal parrot, I think my feathers are amazing. Probably too amazing to have evolved by chance. Too sophisticated. Too intricate. Too perfect. And too beautiful.

I spend hours attending to them every day so that I can show them off to the world in their full glory. And I have many different types of feather, each serving a special purpose. For example, I have the short fluffy

ones (which my owner calls 'my undies'). These keep me insulated, rather like miniature eiderdowns. And then there are my wing feathers – long and elongated – with the shaft off-centre so I can create maximum down-draft in the air. My wing feathers also have wonderful interlocking fronds. When my owner runs his fingers through them, and bends them out of shape, their fronds immediately spring back into position, locking together to achieve maximum strength.

There are also my long tail feathers, each with its own growing tip at the end. They have the flexibility to twist and fan out, acting as my aerial rudder, or bending down to reduce speed. And don't ask me how, but all of my unique, beautiful feathers always grow in exactly the right place and with all the right colours. So you see, I'm really quite a work of art.

Next time you find yourself gazing at a bird, don't just think of it as another bunch of old feathers. My feathers are my warmth, my softness, my beauty, my 'action suit' and my special engineering. And above all, they serve as living proof that I was made by the hands of a wonderful, loving Creator.

Who's a pretty boy then?

In His hand is the life of every creature and the breath of all mankind.   (Job: 12:10)

Islands in the Sea

One of my happy pastimes is to read newspapers. Or at least, I do read them for a while until I eventually decide that it's far more fun to chew them up. And so, one day last week, I found myself reading an edition of 'The Parrot Times.' This reported on the human strife taking place in America. And it was a story which made me feel very, very sad. Because the story of humanity is rather like the story of the Earth ....

In the beginning, there was one great continent called Pangea. It was a 'super-continent.' Strong, unified and majestic. But over time, it started to split into two. And then these two halves – Eurasia and Gondwanaland – they fragmented further. Up to the point where one original continent became seven. And soon there were also countless little islands appearing in the oceans and the seas. Standing apart from all of the other land forms in a kind of 'insular' independence. Proud, defiant, and arrogant: each one believing that it was superior to all of the others around them.

And so it came to pass with humanity. An 'island mentality' has so often led to an intolerance of different customs, cultures, religions and skin colour. And it's even affected the Christian Church. Out of one original church have come more than 40 major divisions, and over 30,000 separate denominations. Rather like a vast scattering of islands. And on occasions, the divide between those islands has been immense. Just think of the history of the Catholics and Protestants ....

Difference is fine. After all, there are all kinds of different parrots! Yes, difference is fine so long as it doesn't degenerate into violence and strife, hatred and discrimination. Because when it sinks to that level, it becomes a self-fulfilling prophecy. A maelstrom of anger, resentment and conflict. It's happened so many times throughout the history of humanity. There have been so many needless wars and acts of violence, harm and cruelty towards others. No wonder God had to send Jesus – His very own Son – to give humanity a way out of the mess.

America is in a great mess right now. And the way out of it will never be achieved through violence and force. No, America needs to put Jesus at the very heart of its troubles. To instil love into the middle of the hatred; humility into the midst of the arrogance; unity into the very heart of the discord; compassion into the midst of the anger. And the peace of the Holy Spirit into the very core of the violence. Jesus can do this if humans allow Him to. But will they? Well, yes they can. There really are examples of hope out there. Even in a vast city like Miami, where a group of American police officers knelt down to pray with a group of protestors in a spontaneous act of peace and harmony.

We're all living in the same world. It's the same water that laps upon the shores of each island and land mass. All of us face the same challenges and difficulties of everyday life. And the peace and love that most of us crave comes not from humanity, but from living with Jesus in our hearts ....

Do not waste time bothering whether you 'love' your neighbour; act as if you do, and you will presently come to love him. (C.S. Lewis: *Mere Christianity*)

Love your neighbour as yourself.

(Mat. 22:39b;
Mark 12:31b;
Luke 10:27b)

Is Life Fair?

A parrot friend of mine told me a story last week which I'd like to share with you.

A man went into a pet shop to buy a parrot. The shopkeeper pointed to three identical-looking parrots sitting in a row on a perch. They'd come from a local firm of lawyers which was in the process of cutting costs. He said: 'The one on the left costs £500.00.'

'Why so expensive?' asked the customer. The owner replied: 'This parrot knows how to do legal research.'

The customer then asked about the next parrot in the line, and was told that it would cost £1,000.00, because it could do everything that the first parrot could, plus knew how to write briefs that would win any legal case. So the increasingly startled customer enquired about the third parrot, and was told that it had a price-tag of £4000.00. So he asked: 'What can it do then?' To which the shopkeeper replied: 'I've never seen him do anything, but the other two call him "the Senior Partner"'.

Our world isn't always very fair, is it? Some of us can work really hard but don't always get our just desserts. Others cruise through life – rather like the third parrot – and yet they somehow come out on top of the pile. At least, from a worldly perspective. But this isn't the case in Heaven where the complete opposite applies. Jesus reminds us that in Heaven …

… the last will be first, and the first will be last.   (Matthew 20:16).

So who do we really work for? For our boss? For the organization that employs us? Or for God? The Book of Colossians answers this rather well:

> Whatever you do, work at it with all your heart, as though you were working for the Lord and not for men. Remember that the Lord will give you as a reward what he has kept for his people. For Christ is the real Master you serve.
> (Colossians 3:23–24. *Amended slightly for flow*)

Is There Life in Lockdown?

As a parrot, whether in this house or out in the wilds, it's a beautiful thing to open up my wings and fly! To fly to wherever the wind or my inclination takes me. My wings are an expression of freedom. I know that humans have legs that they can plod around on, but it's not quite the same.

But right now, humans have to stay at home under a state of lockdown, and that must be so difficult for you all. Suddenly, the freedom that you once enjoyed and took for granted has been put on hold. All because of a microscopic virus. Something so tiny, yet so powerful, that it's knocked your lives out of their normal orbit.

Whether you like it or not, the current lockdown forces everyone to live with more humility. Because you have to comply with the new rules and regulations imposed by your government and health experts. And we'll be breaking the law if we fail to comply.

God's world also comes with some rules and regulations which make humility central to our way of living. And just as with the virus restrictions, God's rules are to protect us from ourselves and others. And perhaps, most worryingly of all, to protect others from ourselves.

As one Italian pastor recently put it: *'Anything is a blessing that shows me my own arrogance.'*

Life in lockdown is never going to be easy. It's tough; it's challenging; it's frustrating; it's hardship. But what will it eventually lead to, apart from the containment of the virus…?

No flowers wear so
Lovely a blue as those
Which grow at the foot of
A glacier; no stars gleam
So brightly as those which
Glisten in the polar sky;
No water tastes so sweet as
That which springs amid
The desert sand; and no faith is so precious as that
Which lives and triumphs in adversity.

(Charles Spurgeon: 1898–1963.
Influential British Baptist Preacher)

It's not the good times which shape us. It's how we approach adversity which counts for everything. Sometimes, it's the effort of battling through which forces us to open up the dingy doors of our hearts; so that God can step inside to do His work. And it's only then that we start to blossom and flourish with a new vibrant energy, just as we were always meant to ….

Hardships often prepare ordinary people for an extraordinary destiny.

(C.S. Lewis: 1898–1963.
British writer, lay theologian and academic)

Keeping Hold of What Really Matters

As I was sitting on my favourite perch one morning, pondering my latest theories of astrophysics and biodynamics, it occurred to me that the more complicated we make this world, the more we tie ourselves up in knots. The more that we discover, the more that we find still needs to be discovered. The deeper we go, the more we shut ourselves off from the relevant and the obvious. And when this happens, we can lose touch with God.

Just think of all of the geniuses throughout history. (Naturally I'm too modest to call myself a genius. I'll let others do that). I mean geniuses like Einstein, Galileo, Aristotle and Darwin.

I'm not sure that their scientific work ever brought them happiness. And so I pose the question .... Do we really need to know about how life evolved or how old the universe is, or how to clone monkeys, humans, or maybe even parrots? Science is all very stimulating and fascinating, but ultimately, will it save our souls? Can mathematical formulas or complex theories teach us about love and compassion, or how we can get to Heaven? The God I know is the God of small and simple things. The God of acts of kindness. The God of smiles. The God of giving. The God of caring. The God of praying for others. And the God of feathers.

We'll probably never need to know how God created the world and the universe around us. Not when it distracts us from the present and immediate things in our lives. Of course, science has its place in our world – particularly with medical research or anything which makes our existence here on Earth that little safer or more comfortable. But science must never become all-consuming. After all, none of us are here for very long. We're born (or hatched). We live. We die. And during that tiny fragment of time in-between, we need to discover God and secure our place in Heaven. And we don't need to be a genius to do that. It's not always about what we pack into our brains. It's more about what we give out from our hearts while we can ....

What good is it for someone to gain the whole world, and yet lose or forfeit their very self?
(Luke 9:25)

Set your minds on things above, not on earthly things. (Colossians 3:2)

Living, Evolving and Improving

It came as quite a shock to me when I discovered that my beautiful feathers are supposed to have evolved from dinosaur scales. This is probably why my owner calls me 'Pterodactyl Midgetus' when I'm flying around above his head.

But you know, it's not where we've come from that matters. It's all about who we are now and where we are heading. That's what interests God! Consider that splendid human, Justin Welby – the Archbishop of Canterbury. He may well be descended from some Neolithic savage, but that doesn't stop him from being a really good fellow. You see, God wants every generation to be better than the last. A kind of moral and social advancement that over time, will see this world become a much better place for all. A world in which the son of a murderer can become a parish priest, or the daughter of a drug baron can become a brilliant foster mother. And we all have a role to play in this advancement. Through acceptance. Through encouragement. And through love.

Parrots aren't really that different to humans. We need to be understood. We need to receive kindness. We need to be given a chance. And above all, we need to be loved. And then you'll start to see us in our full glory.

But there is one big problem with the advancement of humankind. And that's its obsession with money, guns and the annihilation of the natural world around them. Because humanity has evolved in so many ways, yet it's wanton destruction of the natural world around them (and in some cases, themselves) harks back to very primitive times. There is still so much evolving that humans need to do before it's all too late. Otherwise, they will eradicate all life and themselves in the process. And this has all come about because the rate at which they have evolved from primitive beings has failed to keep pace with the rapid development of their modern technology. In other words, they are not mature enough to take responsibility for what they have created. The gun. The chainsaw. The bulldozer. All in a world that's driven by money. But the real 'million dollar' question is whether there's still time for humanity to advance further and change for the better. Or is the human race too backward for that, and therefore doomed?

Our world will never again be a Garden of Eden. But it could be so much better than it is. While there is still life on our planet, none of us must stop evolving. And to evolve effectively, we need to let the essence of God enter our hearts and minds. We are all a part of God's creation. We are all in this life together. It doesn't matter whether you have a beak or a nose, a crest or a perm – let's make our existence better, together (and hopefully) forever – by putting God's love at the centre of all we think and do.

> For the Lord is good and His love endures for ever;
> His faithfulness continues through all generations.
> **(Psalm 100:5)**

Living with the Holy Spirit

Every morning, my owner takes me across to see Nanna who lives in an annexe on the other side of the house. He helps her to get out of bed and get dressed, and then gives her some breakfast. And I usually sit on a door and offer some parrot supervision. But the other day, our little routine came to a shuddering halt. Because 94 year old Nanna let out a dreadful moan, and then collapsed into deep unconsciousness. Her face and mouth contorted into a strange shape. This was clearly more than a faint. And my owner immediately feared the worst....

He quickly dialled '999'. And I listened in to the conversation that followed.

> 'Is the patient conscious?'
> 'No.'
> 'Is the patient breathing?'
> 'I'm not sure. If she is, it's very shallow!'

On hearing this, the operator's voice took on a new intensity. 'Sir, if there's defibrillator in your village, I'd advise you to get it now.'

> 'I'm on my own in the house and supporting my mother.
> I don't think I should leave her.'

Well, actually, my owner wasn't really alone in the house. And I'm not including myself here. No, you see, in the midst of the crisis, he sensed God's presence. And he was convinced that he was in the process of handing over Nanna to God's safe keeping. Nanna has a number of underlying health problems, so resuscitation might not have been in her best interests. Running off and leaving her to get a defibrillator wouldn't have been fair. This was the moment of Nanna's 'hand-over' ....

A full five minutes had passed when Nanna let out a tiny moan. She was still deeply unconscious, but suddenly this was a sign of life. The minutes passed. The operator continued to give words of advice and encouragement, until eventually, after more than ten minutes had passed, an ambulance arrived. And then, quite astonishingly, Nanna began to regain consciousness. For my owner, it was rather like witnessing a kind of resurrection. It turned out that she hadn't had a stroke; nor had her heart valves finally given up. The lengthy black-out was a mystery, but possibly some form of prolonged fit. Well, Nanna slept for the rest of that day, and has since returned to being her old self. Looking back, you could say that this incident put my owner's faith very much to the test. Because it would have been a much worse situation had he not sensed the presence of God alongside him in that room. And had he not believed that Nanna was destined for Heaven ....

This little drama showed how important it is for us to have built a relationship with God, long before a crisis comes our way. So that we don't feel totally on our own. So that we don't feel that death is the end of everything. And so that we don't feel all is lost ....

I don't know how long my morning visits to Nanna will carry on for. But I'll enjoy them every day and be grateful while they last. And when the time finally comes for her to go to Heaven, my owner and I will simply hand everything over to God ....

Peace I leave with you; my peace I give you. I do not give to you as the world gives. Do not let your hearts be troubled and do not be afraid.
(John 14:27)

Now faith is being sure of what we hope for and certain of what we do not see.
(Hebrews 11:1)

And I will ask the Father, and He will give you another Counsellor to be with you for ever – the (Holy) Spirit of Truth. The world cannot accept Him, because it neither sees Him nor knows Him. But you know Him, for He lives with you and will be in you.
(John 14:16–17)

Lost and Found

My human family, like many others, is very good at mislaying things. And this is particularly true of Nanna who lives on the other side of the house. Sometimes it's her walking stick that mysteriously disappears. Other times it's her glasses or her hearing aids. And without any one of these things, she's completely lost. She isn't 'whole' anymore. So the rest of the family joins in a frantic search until the missing item is found. And then it's smiles and relief all round!

You know, God doesn't like losing things either, especially humans and the wonders of His creation. Because we're all very special to Him. We're both loved and wanted by God, even when we don't know it. And that's because we all form a part of God's family. The Bible tells us that there's a special place for humans at His table. And if someone wanders off or gets lost, or simply forgets about Him, then the family of God becomes incomplete.

It was like this for the 18th century clergyman, John Newton. Before handing over his life to God, he'd made a good living out of the slave trade. It was his full-blown 'career' until several close brushes with death (including a dramatic shipwreck), led him to completely change his life around. Later on, in 1779, after having become a clergyman, he wrote the lyrics to one of the greatest hymns of all time – *Amazing Grace*. And for many of us, one line stands out over and above the rest:

'I once was lost, but now am found.'

Of course, we are all sinners. Every single one of us. There are times in our lives when we get things wrong, or wander off or rebel against our Creator. But the Gospels tell us that God's love and grace is so great, that we will always be welcomed back into the fold if we truly regret what we've done.

I tell you that in the same way there will be more rejoicing in heaven over one sinner who repents than over ninety-nine righteous people who do not need to repent.   (Luke 15:7)

So whenever we fall from grace, God's love and forgiveness are there to serve as our safety net. There's no point in us going through life weighed down by heavy burdens of guilt and regret. Not when we can simply swallow our pride, hand over our guilt, and offer up our lives to God so that He can use us in His own special way. For God's love and grace are beyond comprehension. And they are readily available to all of us ....

Repent, then, and turn to God, so that your sins may be wiped out ...
(Acts 3:19a)

Making that Leap of Faith

There are some days when I wake up feeling very energetic. And that's when I can become a bit of a parrot dare-devil. Instead of flying from one perch to another, or taking a casual stroll between the two, I choose to launch into a flying leap. Usually, I make it, but occasionally, I end up in a crumpled heap of feathers on the floor.

As we go through life, there are times when we all have to make a leap of faith. For example, when a young bird first leaves the nest. Or when humans climb on board a plane and depend upon the pilot for their safety. Or when they start a new job or get married. Or when they go into hospital for surgery. In the human world, making a leap of faith is all about relinquishing control; it's about handing over your fate and well-being to someone else. And humans can find that very difficult.

My owner has a friend who has just made a giant leap of faith. Because he needed major brain surgery to save his life. And he was forced to hand over everything that makes him what he is, into the hands of a specialist surgeon. A very skilled surgeon, but someone that he was only able to meet on one occasion beforehand. That took incredible courage. But David is an incredible fellow with a rock-solid faith.

Sometimes, walking into a church for the very first time, saying your first ever prayer out loud, or committing yourself to a Christian journey – these things can all be rather like handing yourself over to a surgeon. Because you have to accept that you're not invincible. That you'll never be the ultimate master of your own fate.

> But man, despite his riches, does not endure; he is like the beasts that perish. This is the fate of those who trust in themselves ... . (Psalm 49:12–13a)

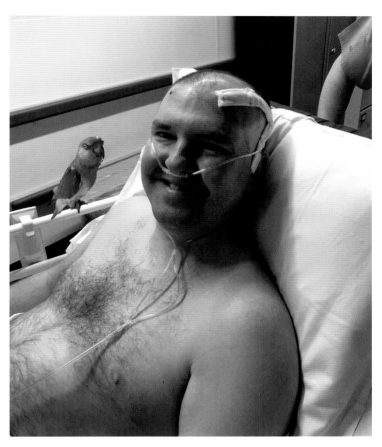

David is a shining example of someone full of
Christian faith, and it's enabled him to come through
so much adversity in his life. He has found God, and
totally trusts Him, come what may. And he's usually
done so with an inner sense of peace and calm....

> ... but the mind controlled by the spirit is (filled with)
> life and peace.   (Romans 8:6b)

Of course, my own leaps of faith from perch to perch
are purely a bit of parrot fun. But when in the future,
things aren't quite so good for me and a crisis comes my
way, I'll be thinking of David. Oh yes, David Campbell,
you're a source of inspiration in a troubled world!

Manna from Heaven

My human owner has to change my water pot every day, or else it ends up as 'parrot soup.' I like to drop tasty morsels into it to soften them up, but then I go away and forget about them.

I've only become this casual about my food because I've never had to worry about it. Thanks to my human owner, food simply appears in my food pot, rather like 'manna from Heaven.' And unlike my feathered friends outside, I don't have to search for it, (although I do raid the fruit bowl when no one's looking!)

I'm ashamed to admit that this situation has made me rather wasteful. It seems that the more we have of something, the more we can take it for granted. And that not only applies to food, but also to friendships, our health, our work, our close relationships, our standard of living, and even to having a roof over our heads. In fact, it's far too easy for us all to take our entire existence for granted. And in the long-term, that won't bring us joy or happiness.

Thank you God for another day and for giving me another chance.

Even if we have very little in our lives, we can make ourselves feel so much better by being 'thankful' for what we've got. By being thankful for every single thing that makes our existence here more comfortable, more enjoyable and more secure. And I'm reminded of a married couple who were well into their eighties; every morning when they woke up in their bed together, they used to say a prayer of thanks to God because they were grateful for having the chance of enjoying yet another day together.

Thoughtfulness often goes hand in hand with thankfulness; so many of us need to stop and think about how much we really have in our lives. And hopefully, God and Jesus will feature high up on that list of things ….

> Be joyful always; pray continually; give thanks in all circumstances, for this is God's will for you in Christ Jesus.   (1Thessalonians 5:16–18)

> … always giving thanks to God the Father for everything in the name of our Lord Jesus Christ. (Ephesians 5:20)

> And whatever you do, whether in word or deed, do it all in the name of the Lord Jesus, giving thanks to God the Father through him.
>   (Colossians 3:17)

Miraculous Mothers: Celebrating Mother's Day

I reckon my mother had a fairly easy time of it. Because I was neatly delivered into this world inside an egg. She then had to sit on me for 28 days before I eventually hatched out. After two and a half weeks, my eyes opened. I fledged at nine weeks and became totally independent after twelve. So the whole process of bringing me into the world and looking after me only lasted for about four months.

It's a rather different story for human mothers. Just imagine having a baby inside you for nine long months! The inconvenience of it all! No glasses of gin or wine for all that time! And then the babies rarely come out as easily as an egg. But that's just the start of it.

Human mothers then spend the next two years teaching their children to stand up, walk and to talk, followed by another sixteen years of telling them to sit down, sit still and be quiet! And all this time, these human mothers are quietly having to evolve. Multi-tasking means that they suddenly have to sprout four sets of arms and hands. And not only that. A load of extra eyes appear on the back of their heads as they try to maintain some semblance of peace, law and order. (Oh dear! Four sets of arms and eyes all round. Am I writing this piece about human mothers or tarantula spiders?)

Anyway, on top of all this, mums have to develop sixth and seventh senses to know what's going on. They have to learn to be peacemakers, comforters, first-aiders, dinner ladies, taxi drivers, counsellors, encouragers, helpers and confidants. And the very best mothers achieve all of this on a foundation of unconditional love ....

Miraculous Mothers: Celebrating Mother's Day

This world is full of all sorts of wonderful humans that step into the role of being mothers. Apart from biological mums, there are grannies, older sisters, foster parents, teachers, support workers, nurses and so many others. And the one thing that binds them all together is this extraordinary virtue called 'love'. And so often it's an unconditional love that's beyond the physical, because this type of love is something spiritual. A love that perseveres and keeps going through thick and thin; through the good times and the difficult ones. A selfless love that continues to shine out of tiredness, exhaustion, fatigue and even despair. What kind of love is this? And who does it remind you of?

A mother's pure love is probably the nearest thing we will ever experience here on Earth to the love of Jesus, the love of God and the love of the Holy Spirit. Because true love comes from all three. And that's what makes so many human mothers so very, very special, and why they must never be taken for granted . . . .

> Love is patient, love is kind. It does not envy, it does not boast, it is not proud. It is not rude, it is not self-seeking, it is not easily angered, it keeps no record of wrongs. Love does not delight in evil but rejoices with the truth. It always protects, always trusts, always hopes, always perseveres.
> (1 Corinthians: 13:4–7).

So here's to human mothers and my own feathery one. Happy Mothers' Day to you all! Happy Mothers' Day!

On Your Bike Then!

I recently looked out of the window and saw my family of humans sitting on a collection of round things joined by metal rods. Not only this, but they were using them as a form of self-propulsion. I was so taken aback, that I had to let rip with a spot of head-banging! I later discovered that this strange activity is known as 'riding a bicycle'. And I suppose that if you don't have your own set of wings, it's the next best thing.

And then I remembered these words of Professor Albert Einstein:

Life is like riding a bicycle. To keep your balance, you must keep moving.

(Albert Einstein: 1979–1955.
German born theoretical physicist).

Our Christian journeys are just like that. And there will be times when we grind to a halt and fall off. God and Jesus know that. Of course they do. It may be our own fault, or we may have collided with something in our path. But when we fall off, that isn't the end of it. Far from it. All we're asked to do is to stand up again, dust ourselves down, and then carry on. So that we propel ourselves further along our Christian journeys. Towards God and Jesus and all they represent. Towards love, truth, and compassion. Towards a reason, a purpose, a meaning and a direction. And ultimately, towards eternal life itself.

And all the time, the energy that keeps us moving is faith. Because faith is energy. It never stands still. It's continuous. Faith is all about searching for the answers to the questions and the doubts that we harbour deep inside. About stepping outside the limitations of our five senses. About continuing to believe in what we don't fully understand. So that we continue to propel ourselves towards something that is much bigger, greater, and more wonderful than we can ever know.

Trust in the Lord with all your heart and lean not on your own understanding;

In all your ways acknowledge him and he will make your paths straight.   (Proverbs 3:5–6)

We live by faith, not by sight.   (2 Corinthians 5:7)

Let us rid ourselves of everything that gets in the way, and of the sin which holds on to us so tightly, and let us run with determination the race that lies before us. Let us keep our eyes fixed on Jesus, on whom our faith depends from beginning to end.

(Hebrews 12:1–3. *Amended for flow and clarity*).

Doubt sees obstacles. Faith sees the way. So maybe that's why humans sometimes say to one another: 'On your bike then!'

Parrot Obituaries

Parrots are just as important as people, so why shouldn't there be parrot obituaries? (Do you think that a parrot might have written this opening line?)

Before he acquired me, my owner was reading a parrot magazine when he spotted a parrot obituary near the back. 'How bizarre!' he thought. Wasn't this taking things a little too far?

Of course, I have now put him right on this point. The obituary in question described how 'Percy' used to join his owner in bed for a morning cup of tea,

and then slide down the staircase bannister when she headed downstairs. Percy's party-piece was to strut up and down on the breakfast table with a teaspoon in his beak. And he would show his owner great love and affection by nuzzling into her neck and gently preening her hair. The two of them were inseparable. They'd been together for nearly 40 years, so the sudden passing of Percy was one very major bereavement.

You see, parrots, like most humans, yearn for a life-long companion. Someone that they can love and trust and with whom they can live out their lives. Acquiring a parrot is a bit like getting married. And the pain of a bereavement can be a really terrible thing on both sides.

And so we have to ask the question whether people and parrots will ever be reunited with one another in Heaven? Does the Bible say anything about this? Well indirectly, it does. And it appears to be good news....

> ... creation itself will one day be set free from its slavery to decay and will share the glorious freedom of the children of God.   (Romans 8:19–21)

Would a loving God really allow the people and creatures of His creation to simply shrivel up and turn to dust when they die? Humans like to believe that they're above all other creatures, but the truth is that all living things form a part of the same creation. So these Bible verses give all of us – parrots, people, elephants, Labradors, ponies, penguins and whatever else – a message of real HOPE. It doesn't simply depend upon our level of intelligence. It's who we are, and what we carry inside that counts. So I, for one, believe that Percy and the lady of his life, will one day be reunited!

In his hand is the life of every creature and the breath of all mankind.   (Job 12:10)

Parrots of the Caribbean!

This all sounds like some new movie release, doesn't it? Perhaps the title of a new action-packed film full of swash-buckling Macaws and daring Amazons....

Actually, I'm thinking rather more about the relationship that parrots once enjoyed with the old Caribbean pirates. Parrots have become every bit as synonymous with pirates as eye patches, hooks and false legs. Just think of Long John Silver and his parrot 'Captain Flint' in the book *Treasure Island*.

And our association with pirates doesn't necessarily make us bad. You see, pirates had very few genuine friends, even amongst the crew of their ships. They existed in a cut-throat world of 'dog-eat-dog'. If you were a pirate, then qualities such as trust, loyalty and affection were in very short supply.

(It was rather like being the British Prime Minister during the run-in to Brexit). And quite often, the only true, loyal and dependable companions that they had were their parrots.

We parrots can form incredibly strong bonds with one another, as well as with our human companions. It's one of our endearing qualities. And humans often yearn for friendships and relationships that are full of genuine love, trust and loyalty. They look for someone that will remain by their side through thick and thin. For someone that will stand up for them, care about them, and always be a friend. The old Caribbean pirates discovered these qualities in parrots. And these days, humans search for the same things in their spouses, partners and friends. Some find what they're looking for. Others don't. But what some of us fail to appreciate is that our greatest friend in life is Jesus. By dying on the cross more than 2000 years ago, He was already looking after our interests long before we were ever born.

Deep down, most of us yearn for some stability in our lives. Not just pirates, but the young, the elderly, criminals and law abiders alike. But lasting stability is rarely found in this life. Ultimately, it's only Jesus that can offer us what we need. If not in this world, in the next. And that is why He said these special words to His disciples:

> Do not let your hearts be troubled. Trust in God; trust also in me. In my Father's house there are many rooms; if it were not so, I would have told you. I am going there to prepare a place for you. And if I go and prepare a place for you, I will come back and fetch you, so that you can join me there.
>
> (John 14:1–3. *Amended slightly for flow*).

Parrots, Politics and Presidents

Human politics and parrots don't really mix. After all, parrots can squawk loud enough as it is. We don't need politics to fire us up to reach the loudest decibels.

But it hasn't escaped my notice that there may be a new President heading into the White House, (arguments, lawsuits and legal judgements allowing). In America, they have a kind of shouting competition, and whoever makes the most din usually ends up as President. And I guess that being sent to the White House is rather like being sent to the doghouse in this country, (especially if you're too noisy or stir up too much trouble).

As I sit back on my perch and gently reflect upon the world around me, I see present day America as one enormous football stadium. Inside the stadium are two opposing teams supported by two opposing crowds. And right in the middle of it all there's a desperate referee trying to maintain some order and unity. As in all football matches, there can only be one winner, so that there's total euphoria on one side of the stadium and a sense of utter despair on the other. Oh dear!

Humans should never allow politics to take hold of their entire existence. Of course, you may prefer some Presidents to others, but at the end of the day, Presidents along with their politics are a creation of humanity. That's all they are, and they should never be allowed to block out the light of much greater things that lurk behind. Life should never be about winning the race into the White House. It should be about winning the race into Heaven. About acting upon what really matters and putting things into a true perspective. What's more important? Four more years for Trump? A new start with Biden? Or eternity with Jesus Christ?

The American Presbyterian Minister James H. Aughey said this prior to being assassinated by a political opponent:

> Death to a Christian is the funeral of all his sorrows and evils, and the resurrection of all his joys.
>
> (James H. Aughey: 1828–1911. *American Presbyterian Minister condemned to death by his political opponents, and ultimately assassinated*).

But in order to get to that point, you have to discover true humility. The humility that is so often missing from the world of human politics.

America is crying out for humility and love. So I'd like to leave you with a couple of verses from the book of Titus:

Remind the people to be subject to rulers and authorities, to be obedient, to be ready to do whatever is good, to slander no-one, to be peaceable and considerate, and to show true humility towards all men.
(Titus 3:1–2).

America, these verses were written for you right now ....

Every good thing in the Christian life grows in the soil of humility. Without humility, every virtue and grace withers. That's why Calvin said humility is first, second and third in the Christian faith.
(John Piper: 1946–present. *American pastor and theologian*)..

Powered by Love!

I'm not really a great fan of human politicians, but there is one in particular, who has recently caught my eye. And that might be because Boris Johnson has a hint of Cockatoo about him. But not only that. No. Last week, shortly after being released from Intensive Care, he made one of the most profound statements ever to come from the lips of any politician. Talking about the Coronavirus, he said this:

We will win because our NHS is the beating heart of this country. It is the best of this country. It is unconquerable. It is powered by love.
(Boris Johnson: b. 1964. *Current British Prime Minister*).

And Mr Johnson went on to make a reference to two special nurses – Luis from Portugal, and Jenny from New Zealand, who had remained by his side during his darkest hours in hospital.

And all this made me think back to Martin Luther King, who once spoke these very memorable words:

Workers in our NHS – along with many others that are so often taken for granted – are all continuing to keep our society going out of a sense of duty, care and underlying love. All of these people could so easily quit and walk away, but they haven't, even when it means putting themselves at risk.

We must discover the power of love, the redemptive power of love. And when we discover that, we will be able to make this old world a new world, for love is the only way.
(Martin Luther King: 1929–1968. *American Baptist Minister and Civil Rights Activist assassinated at the age of 39*).

Now, let's turn the clock back a couple of years. To when Prince Harry married Megan Markle in the chapel at Windsor Castle. During the service, the American Pastor, Bishop Michael Curry gave a very powerful address about 'The Power of Love':

And having had his near-death experience in hospital, Boris Johnson knows exactly what these words mean.
Their wisdom. Their power. And their significance for all humanity.

We were made by a power of love, and our lives were meant – and are meant – to be lived in that love. That's why we are here …. There's power in love. There's power in love to help and heal when nothing else can. There's power in love to lift up and liberate when nothing else will. There's power in love to show us the way to live.

(Bishop Michael Curry: 1953–present. *American Bishop and Primate of the Episcopal Church*).

I often think of the NHS (and other caring organisations) as an example of how God wants us all to live our lives throughout the wider world. Because collectively, it represents an expression of God's love. God's love, working through an army of 1.5 million health workers. All tirelessly and selflessly giving of themselves so that others may be helped, comforted or physically saved. A team working together as a huge driving force for goodness and compassion. Made up of people representing every race, colour and creed, drawn from so many different countries around the world. All united by their desire to care, to cure, to fix and to improve, because of an astonishing calling to help humanity. The NHS is not simply a health service. It provides a model for how humans should all be living their lives around the world ….

Love is patient, love is kind. It does not envy, it does not boast, it is not proud. It is not rude, it is not self-seeking, it is not easily angered, it keeps no record of wrongs. Love does not delight in evil but rejoices with the truth. It always protects, always trusts, always hopes, always perseveres.   (1 Corinthian 13:4–7)

Prayers or Bombs?

My owner always lines the bottom of my cage with sheets of newspaper. And I always hope that he uses the 'Puzzles' section as there's nothing I enjoy more than a spot of Sudoku, a word wheel or a quiz. But if I'm really unlucky, I can end up with the 'Politics' pages. Yes, there are some good politicians out there, but there are also many self-centred ones, and there's nothing worse than having their faces staring up at me while I'm sitting on my perch.

And I must admit that there are times when I'm tempted to climb up to my highest perch and use them for 'target practice.'

But then I stop and remember that I'm meant to be a Christian parrot rather than some kind of deranged seagull. So instead of dropping bombs on them, I pray for them. I pray that they will serve others and not just themselves. I pray that they will make decisions based on good morals. And I pray that God can use them for His work.

It can be very hard for us to pray for people that upset us, or whom we simply don't like. But being a Christian is all about turning negative thoughts into positive action for God. Praying for the family member that you haven't spoken to for years. Praying for the person at work that makes your life a misery. And praying for all of the bullies and dictators and thugs of this world.

Positive prayer creates positive energy. Build that energy up enough and it can result in positive change. Astonishing, amazing, unexpected change. And that is the power of faith through prayer .…

But I tell you: love your enemies, and pray for those who persecute you .… (Matthew 5:44)

Therefore confess your sins … and pray for one another .… (James 5:16a)

Show proper respect to everyone .… (1 Peter 2:17a)

Do nothing out of selfish ambition or vain conceit, but in humility consider others better than yourselves. (Philippians 2:3)

Bear with each other and forgive whatever grievances you may have against one another. (Colossians 3:13a)

Pterodactyl Midgetus!

For a spot of bedtime reading last night, I thought I'd look at an old copy of the 'Journal of Molecular Biology'. It's an old favourite amongst parrots, and a fascinating read it was too! It was all about how a human called Professor Chuong (based in Southern California) had

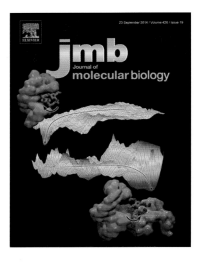

successfully carried out experiments to prove that feathers originate from dinosaur scales. It's quite mind-blowing to think that some hard, dull, rigid plates of keratin can evolve into something that's as beautiful, soft and iridescent as me!

For some reason, there are still a lot of humans that don't believe in the theory of evolution. In America, polls suggest that only 39% of humans do so. (Perhaps it's because humans don't have their very own set of feathers!)

And yet I believe that evolution is a key part of God's plan for us all – especially if you're a human. And at two levels. Firstly, there's evolution spread over many millions of years that sees creatures like me adapt and adjust to their surroundings. That's the process identified by Charles Darwin.

But more importantly, there is the process of evolution which takes place during our individual lifetimes. As we go through life, we grow, we learn, we age and we change. So that at the time of our passing, we are quite different to how we started out. Especially if our passage through life involves a Christian journey. A journey from the physical to the spiritual. From Earth to Heaven. From humanity to God.

Usually, our transformation is slow and gradual. But on other occasions, it can be spectacular and dramatic. Just think of Saul's transformation on the road to Damascus (Acts 9).

The bottom line is that we should never find ourselves standing still. God wants us to change and to evolve for the better. And Jesus has to remind His disciples about this when they bicker about which of them will be the greatest in Heaven:

> And He said: 'I tell you the truth, unless you change and become like little children, you will never enter the Kingdom of Heaven'.   (Matthew 18:3)

I know I'll never be perfect. I'll always want to be the most beautiful bird in town or gnaw things that I shouldn't. But when the time comes for me to finally fall off my perch, I hope that I'll be close enough to knock on God's door and say: 'I've changed. I'm Yours now. And this is where I want to be.'

Receiving Gifts

As we get ever closer to Christmas Day, humans are thinking more and more about gifts. Because at Christmas time, they have a tradition of giving one another presents. And I usually get something too. It might be an irresistible parrot treat, or something for me to chew up and destroy.

So Christmas is a time of giving. But what about the receiving part? How easy do we find it to accept the gifts of others? And are we even grateful that somebody's thought of us?

A wife once decided to cook her husband a tasty meal. She slaved for three hours in her kitchen, trying out a new recipe, while her husband was out, socialising with his friends. And he failed to return home at the time they'd agreed. So, feeling frustrated, she rang him and said that if he wasn't back in ten minutes, she'd give the entire meal to their pet dog. Well, within three minutes flat, and totally breathless, the man sprinted in through the front door shouting 'Is the dog still ok?'

But gratitude is only half of the story. Because so many humans feel uncomfortable about accepting a special gift or an act of kindness from somebody else. And so often it's because they want to be independent or self-sufficient. They want to be strong enough to exist without the help and support of others. A bit like the all-action heroes in many Hollywood blockbusters. Rambo, Superman, Wonder Woman and the rest. But having this mindset is denying the reality of Life. Because all humans, like all creation, are ultimately vulnerable, fragile and needy. And perhaps no more so than when they're confronting death.

The truth is that to survive, to grow and to prosper, we all have to learn how to *receive* as well as how to give. So many humans are obsessed with hiding their inner frailties, and so often, that's down to pride. It's only when we learn to have some humility that we can begin to get rid of the façade, and start to accept the gifts of others, (including God), who want nothing more than to help us.

For God so loved the world that He gave His one and only Son, so that whoever believes in Him shall not perish but have eternal life …
(John 3:16)

There's an old human saying that's 'It's better to give than to receive.' But that's wrong. Because both are equally important. For until we learn to receive, we can never appreciate the gift of Jesus. True love *gives* while humility *receives*. Both are a part of the essence of Jesus ….

95

Seeing it All from a Different Angle...

Not everything in Life is quite as it seems. Or else things don't turn out to be quite as we expected. The problem is that we like to believe that we know far more than we really do. About all kinds of things ranging from politics to single mothers, and from rough sleeping through to the pros and cons of Brexit. You name it, and we'll have an opinion about it. And we can easily fall into the trap of becoming self-appointed experts on just about anything and everything around us. Even when our knowledge and understanding of the world is very limited. After all, most of us only view it all from one particular angle. Let me give you an example.

Neil Armstrong is a superhero amongst humans, because he was the very first man to walk on the moon. Back in 1969, as he stepped out of his lunar module for the very first time, many humans wondered whether he'd come face to face with a real-life alien! But at the precise moment of his first lunar step, there was only one alien on the surface of the moon, and that was Neil Armstrong. And to prove my point, all you have to do is take his first name 'Neil' and the first letter of his surname, (the 'A'), then join them together and read them backwards!! You see, it's all about our perception of things.

Or if you choose to turn around the 'evil' in your life, then you can really start to 'live'. And when Mary gave birth to Jesus in the stable, some folk felt He was reducing Himself to the level of a 'dog'. But He was definitely no 'dog'. Because this Jesus proved to be the Son of 'God'.

Our whole perception of the things we encounter is very often flawed, and many of us are too narrow or stubborn to change. The Pharisees persecuted Jesus because they were not prepared to consider any alternative viewpoint to their own. So healing people on the Sabbath was strictly forbidden. And surely the real Son of God wouldn't spend time socialising with sinners, outcasts, the poor and the sick instead of rubbing shoulders with the rich, the powerful, and 'the virtuous'! And why die on a cross to save the very people that were causing Him so much suffering and torment? Jesus has always had a habit of shattering our expectations and spinning our perceptions around a full 180 degrees.

Sometimes, (and I stress – sometimes) when something bad happens to us such as a redundancy or a bout of ill-health, a bankruptcy or the break-up of a relationship, it can prove to be a blessing in disguise. Because it may be about to steer us on a new course bringing us closer to God and Jesus.

Some humans think of me as a 'parrot genius' because of my writing and my philosophical thoughts. But the truth is this: the further I travel on this journey called Life, the more I come to realise how little I really know. It's the same for all of us. And for that reason, we all need to carry humility in our hearts. Because humility allows us to be shaped and directed by God. Without it, we may stumble and fall. We could give ourselves up to the *'devil'* when we could have really *'lived'*. Or become one of the *'rats'* in the gutter when we could have been a *'star'* in God's eyes.

One thing I do know,
I was blind
but now I see!
            (John 9:25b)

... the people living
in darkness have
seen a great light
        (Matthew 4:16a)

So the question for all of us is this: which way round are we reading these words? Which way round are we perceiving the world? Allowing God inside us is like going to the opticians. Because we end up seeing what was previously hidden or blurred....

Small is Beautiful

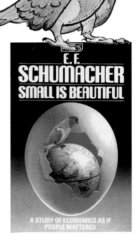

I rather like this title because it could easily describe me! You don't have to be a large Amazon or a dashing Macaw to have good looks and stunning colours. Pocket-sized parrots can be just as good!

Sadly, this page isn't about me at all. No, the title's borrowed from a famous collection of essays published in 1973 by the economist Ernst Friedrich Schumacher. At the time, it was quite a revolutionary book because most human economists believed that 'big was best' and 'the bigger, the better!' But 'Small is Beautiful' challenged that belief, and went on to become a huge best seller.

And in so many ways, the title 'Small is Beautiful' applies to the Christian faith as well. Because you don't have to be big and powerful to serve God well. You don't have to be an Archbishop of Canterbury, a Mother Teresa, a Pope or even a local Vicar. Nor does God expect us all to set up wonderful new charities, or build brand new mission hospitals around the world…

> Not all of us can do great things. But we can do small things with great love.
>
> (Mother Teresa: 1910–1997.
> *Catholic missionary posthumously made a Saint*)

And a small thing can be as simple as offering one small act of kindness every day. Keep it up, and that's seven acts of kindness per week. Or 30 per month. Or 365 per year. Or 3650 per decade. And maybe even 25,000 throughout an entire lifetime. Small acts of kindness can seem insignificant at the time, but they soon add up. Multiply that across an entire population, and just think how different our world would be!

98

The Coronavirus pandemic has forced so many humans to look afresh at the lives they lead. To consider what's important. What really brings them joy and happiness. And what really nourishes the inner soul. And so often, it's the little things which count. So small acts of kindness and love should be part of our daily routine ....

So, never feel small, unimportant or worthless. Because day by day, you can do something wonderful for God. 'Small' can really be 'beautiful'!

Do what you can, with what you have, where you are ....
(Theodore Roosevelt: 1858–1919.
Former US President)

Every man is guilty of all the good he didn't do.
(Voltaire: 1694–1778.
French writer, historian and philosopher)

What counts in life is not the mere fact that we have lived. It is the difference we have made to the lives of others ....
(Nelson Mandela: 1918–2013. *Former South African President and anti-apartheid activist*)

As He looked up, Jesus saw the rich putting their gifts into the temple treasury. He also saw a poor widow put in two very small copper coins. 'I tell you the truth,' He said, 'this poor widow has put in more than all of the others. All these people gave their gifts out of their wealth; but she out of her poverty put in all she had to live on'.
(Luke 21: 1–4)

That All Important 'Welcome'

My owner is a very strange kind of human. He does all kinds of weird things, and his condition always gets worse during the run-in to Christmas. Last month, he put out more than fifty light-up animals in the front garden! Fortunately, my blushes were spared because he couldn't get hold of a light-up parrot. But even so, there's still a flock of light-up flamingos out there!

Then, the other day, he suddenly appeared in the house with a church. Not a real one of course, but a 'light-up' church as part of his array of indoor Christmas decorations. When I first laid eyes on it, I thought 'Oh no!' Because unlit, it simply looked like a large chunk of worthless plastic. But after he plugged it in, and the lights came on, I had to agree that it looked rather nice. In fact, it looked warm and inviting.

And very begrudgingly, I have to admit that he's probably 'hit' on something here, (even if he doesn't realise it). Because the image that a real church projects to its surrounding community is so important. A large, dark, imposing building with narrow, dingy windows, will never encourage new humans to walk in through its doors. And the welcome that everyone receives on the other side of those doors is just as important. It needs to be bright and uplifting. Warm and friendly. Relaxed and inclusive. For every church of God must welcome everyone, whoever they may be, if they walk in off the street with good intentions in their heart.

And maybe some churches need to put up a banner outside to say just that. Something along the lines of: 'Welcome! Come inside. Come and join the Sinner's Club. Paupers, parrots and politicians included!'

The Bible has quite a lot to say about this:

> Accept one another, then, just as Christ accepted you ... .
> (Romans 15:7).

> Do not forget to entertain strangers, for by so doing some people have entertained angels without knowing it.
> (Hebrews 13:2).

> There is neither Jew nor Greek, slave nor free, male nor female, for you are all one in Jesus Christ. (Galatians 3:28)

Sometimes, when someone walks in through the door of a church for the very first time, only God can see their full potential. But it's the role of every church to welcome those folk, and to allow them to blossom according to God's will. And that will always happen, so long as the church is something more than a large piece of plastic...

The Albino Parrot

Just like humans, parrots can easily get bored. There's always a fine balance in life between not doing too much, and not doing too little every single day. Bored parrots can start to pull their feathers out. Or to gnaw things that they shouldn't. And I guess this is where I need to make a confession.

When I was a young bird, my owner was away for long hours each day working in London. And not surprisingly, I got bored. He allowed me to fly free in his kitchen while he was missing. So, one day, I decided to gnaw the door of one of the kitchen cupboards. In fact I didn't just gnaw it. I went right through it, excavating a kind of nest hole.

Once inside the cupboard, I discovered all kinds of interesting things, including three full packets of flour. And of course, I had a wonderful time. When my owner returned home that evening, he discovered that I'd turned into an albino parrot. And as for the cupboard – well – it wasn't quite how it used to be.

Fortunately, because of our bond, my owner forgave me, but afterwards, I was no longer allowed to roam free in the kitchen on my own. You see, too much time on your hands can be a bad thing for parrots. And it can be a bad thing for humans as well. There can be too much time for humans to stress and worry. Or too much time for them to consume drugs and alcohol. Or too much time for them to gamble away their money, or to go shopping to buy things that they don't really need. Or too much time for them to fuss about their looks or their health.

Life is too short for all of this. We only get one chance at life here on Earth, so we need to make the most of it. But not so that we are frantic and burn ourselves out by doing too much. As with most things in life, it's all about striking a happy balance. Discovering what's right for each of us as unique individuals.

Jesus never intended us to be idle. He warned the people of His day about wasting their lives by focusing on the wrong kind of work, or not working at all. In the Gospel of John, He says:

> Do not work for food that spoils, but for food that endures to eternal life, which the Son of Man will give you.
> (John 6:27)

Our ultimate work here on Earth is to walk the pathway that leads to Heaven. That's our real work. If we do nothing, or we use up our time doing the wrong things, then we will be trekking up the wrong path. For example, gnawing through the doors of kitchen cabinets . . . .

But there's a lot more to it than this. Opportunities will come along that we need to grab hold of and embrace. Think about the story of Martha and Mary described in Luke chapter 10. When Jesus visits their house, Mary realizes that this is a once in a lifetime opportunity to listen to and learn from Jesus. Martha meanwhile, is out the back preparing food for their guests and misses everything Jesus has to say. And she scolds Mary for not helping her. But actually, Mary was progressing along the road to Heaven while Martha was remaining static.

God's work for humans (and parrots!) comes in all shapes and forms. So which road are we walking? The one that leads to Heaven or the road that goes to nowhere?

'Martha, Martha,' the Lord answered, 'you are worried and upset about many things, but only one thing is needed. Mary has chosen what is better . . . .'
(Luke 10:41–42a)

The Art of Building Bridges

I'm a very tame bird, so I usually only fly when I've got some energy to burn. Otherwise I tend to move around different rooms by using improvised bridges. For example, the clothes airer, a window sill, the back of a sofa, or a curtain rail – they all come in very handy. And it's a more leisurely way to travel!

Of course, humans are very clever because they can build their own special bridges to get across rivers and valleys and estuaries. There was once a human in the UK called Isambard Brunel who was particularly good at it. But you don't have to earn a degree in engineering to become an effective bridge-builder. Far from it. Because the Christian life is all about building bridges in all walks of life. Bridges between humanity and God. Bridges between different races and cultures and religions. And bridges between those that have fallen out.

Just think of how Jesus bridged all of the different sections of society during His time here on Earth. He didn't just mingle with the rich, the Romans and the Pharisees.

No, He spent so much of His time amongst the tax collectors, the drop-outs and those at the bottom end of society. Amongst lepers, sinners and the much-despised Samaritans. And amongst women as well as men.

Jesus knew that society can only move forwards when it builds firm bridges. But a bridge can only be built when two sides are prepared to meet in the middle. Otherwise, the whole thing will come crashing down, and the world will take a backward step.

The Bible has a great deal to say about unity and reconciliation ....

The ultimate bridge builder was never Isambard Brunel. It was Jesus Christ. Because by coming to Earth and dying on the cross, He single-handedly bridged the greatest gap in existence – the expanse between Heaven and Earth. And unlike my clothes airer or the curtain rail, there is nothing improvised about Jesus' bridge. It'll stand the test of time because it's built to last for ever. And one day, I will strut my stuff along the length of it and never look back!

Bear with each other and forgive whatever grievances you may have against one another. Forgive as the Lord forgave you .... (Colossians 3:13)

How good and pleasant it is when brothers live together in unity! (Psalm 133:1)

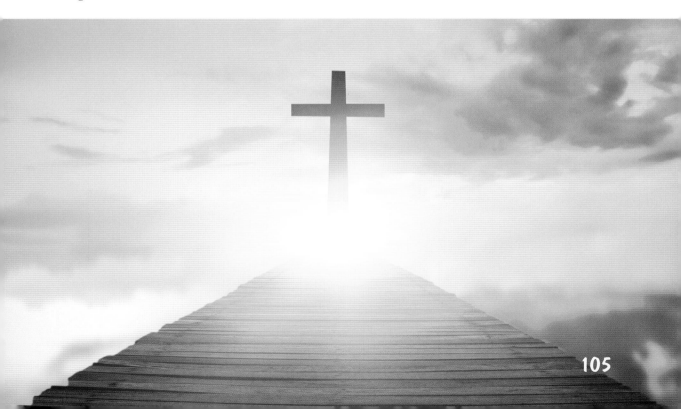

The Banishment of Gregory Peck

I recently read an article about human bullying. Yes, it said that 'bullying is the manifestation of a primitive need to become the leader of the pack. The modern-day bully believes he is a human being, but he is really behaving like an animal'. I had to chuckle because recent events in the garden rather proved this point!

Earlier in the week, a new pheasant moved into town. Or to be more precise, into the front garden. He was an extra-large bird and a 'loner'. He didn't mix with any of his fellow-kind; the others all stayed away from him, keeping to the back garden. And 'Gregory Peck', as he became known, certainly didn't want to mix with my owner.

It all began with Gregory Peck chasing my owner's car up and down the lane outside. Then things went from bad to worse. While the car was parked in the driveway, he'd sit on its roof, waiting for my owner to come out of the front door. Then he'd fly at him, lashing out with his beak and spurs in a frenzied attack. Soon, my owner could only exit the front door if he was armed with an umbrella for self-defence.

Then one day, my owner joined me in the kitchen to wash the dishes. Suddenly, there came a loud 'crash' at the window, and there sitting on the windowsill the other side of the glass was Gregory Peck himself, (with a malevolent look in his eye!). He pecked the window and stormed up-and-down trying to get in for

an attack! Things were now very much out of control. So my human family hatched a plan. My owner was used as 'the human bait'. And while Gregory Peck was busy attacking him outside, the rest of the family sneaked up behind and threw an old blanket over him, bundled him up, and placed him inside a box. After a little drive, Gregory Peck was released to begin a new life in a field of his own. And peace has been restored.

The Bible is full of stories of aggressors and troublemakers who are eventually brought to heel. In his prophecy against Moab, Isaiah predicts how:

> The oppressor will come to an end, and destruction will cease; the aggressor will vanish from the land. (Isaiah 16:4a)

And there's a clear moral to our story of Gregory Peck. For if he'd only tried to fit in and live like the other pheasants in the back garden, he'd have enjoyed a good life of relative ease and comfort. He'd have been fed each day and existed in a place where pheasants were safe from being shot or runover. But because of his bad behaviour, he brought about his own downfall, and was banished.

All humanity and creation should, officially, be banished from Heaven. That would certainly be the case had Jesus not died on the cross to save us all. And the million-dollar question is this. Do we have the humility within us to see this and accept it? Because if not, we are effectively banishing ourselves. And that was never meant to be a part of God's plan ....

> For God so loved the world that He gave His one and only Son, that whoever believes in Him shall not perish but have eternal life. For God did not send His Son into the world to condemn the world, but to save the world through Him. (John 3:16–17)

The Brilliant Science of Sharing

We parrots have a wonderful old saying that goes like this:

'It's easier for a parrot to go through the eye of a needle than for an overfat bird to share its food with others.'

I've often thought about this from two perspectives. Why is it that so many of 'the haves' crave for more and more, even when it's at the expense of others? And how can a parrot go through the eye of a needle in the first place?

Well, to try to answer this second question, I looked through some of my back copies of the *Journal of Molecular Science*. I mean, after all, *how do* you get a Hyacinth Macaw to go through the eye of a needle? Can you get its cells to squeeze up and breathe in a bit, rather like when humans get on board an underground train in the height of the London rush hour? And would they then 'ping back' into shape again afterwards? Humans seem to do it when they disembark at Green Park and Piccadilly Circus. Isn't this world so full of unanswered questions?

As God created the world, nothing will be impossible for Him. And if He so desires, God can pass parrots, camels or anything else through the eye of a needle just like that! But I very much doubt whether human scientists will ever solve the puzzle of how it's done. Humans simply aren't clever enough. Maybe human science should focus on other things that often elude mankind. Such as why human society allows for so much self-interest instead of sharing. Why it tolerates the 'fat bird' mentality that causes the human world to be so horribly imbalanced. Sharing is a scientifically brilliant concept because it can allow everyone to live their lives to their full potential. Sharing knowledge, sharing discoveries, sharing resources, sharing wealth, sharing love and sharing peace. With the end result being a better life for all humanity. But humans have rarely been clever enough to see this. Instead, many have selected the route of short-term greed and long-term self-interest, irrespective of the dire consequences. And as a result of this, today's human world is divided up between 'the haves' and 'the have-nots.' Recent figures reveal that 29.93% of all the worlds' wealth is located in the USA.

Europe has 25.2% and China 17.7%. At the other end of the scale comes India with just 3.5%, the whole of Latin America with 2.7%, and the whole of Africa with just 1.1% (source: https://www.visualcapitalist.com/all-of-the-worlds-wealth-in-one-visualization).

And in the eighteenth century, the great John Wesley was even more outspoken when he preached about self-interest:

> Do you not know that God entrusted you with that money (all above what buys necessities for your families) to feed the hungry, to clothe the naked, to help the stranger, the widow, the fatherless; and, indeed, as far as it will go, to relieve the wants of mankind? How can you, how dare you defraud the Lord by applying it to any other purpose?
>
> (John Wesley: 1703–1791. *Leader of the English Methodist movement*)

Ever since Jesus walked the Earth, Christians have had a great deal to say about this:

> When someone steals another's clothes, we call them a thief. Should we not give the same name to one who could clothe the naked and does not? The bread in your cupboard belongs to the hungry; the coat unused in your closet belongs to the one who needs it; the unused shoes rotting in your closet belong to the one who has no shoes; the money which you hoard belongs to the poor.
>
> (St. Basil the Great: 330–379AD. *Greek Bishop and theologian*)

Today's human world is poles apart from these ideals. If it could only meet somewhere in the middle, the world would be transformed. And this isn't just some scientific theory. It's the raw truth. Which equates to brilliant science ….

> And do not forget to do good and to share with others …. (Hebrews 13:16a)

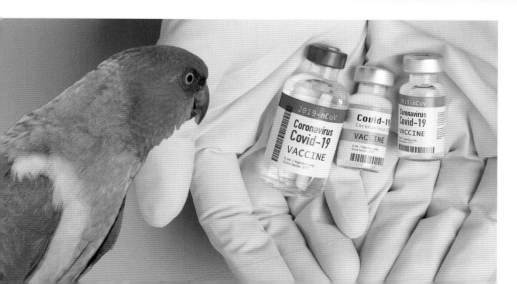

109

The Broccoli, the Mushroom, the Walnut and the Banana

I like to eat virtually anything (especially when it's not being guarded on my owner's plate or in the dog bowl!) And that happens to include broccoli, mushrooms, walnuts and bananas. Which leads me on to this little story . . . .

Four pieces of food were gathered together on a tabletop.

> *The broccoli said: 'I look like a small tree.'*
> *The mushroom said: 'I look like an umbrella.'*
> *The walnut said: 'I look like a brain.'*
> *And the banana said: 'Please can we change the subject?'*

I guess we've all felt a bit like that banana at some stage in our lives. Sometimes embarrassed, sometimes not quite fitting in with others, or simply feeling different or inferior.

It must be like that for humans of different colours, races, cultures or creeds when they find themselves living away from their roots. Or for people walking into a new club or a cliquey church for the very first time. Or it can even happen amongst our friends when we make a careless or insensitive comment.

Humans have invented something called 'political correctness' to try to make everyone feel valued and included. But like many human initiatives, 'political correctness' is usually flawed. Because so often, it's clinically enforced without love, warmth or compassion.

The Broccoli, the Mushroom, the Walnut and the Banana

Ultimately, it's love that will change our society. It's love that will make us all feel comfortable with one another and make us more sensitive towards the feelings of others. It's love that changes attitudes and prejudices and negative mindsets. It's love that makes us all feel valued and accepted, despite who we are and what we look like. Irrespective of whether you're a piece of broccoli, a mushroom, a walnut or a banana. And therefore, love should be at the very heart of everything that we think, believe and do. Right from the top of government, down to the vagrant sleeping rough on the streets. It's only love that can harmonise, pacify and unite. And if you're still in any doubt, just take a look at my cousins, the Lovebirds!

Whoever does not love does not know God, because God is love. (1 John 4:8)

Be completely humble and gentle; be patient bearing with one another in love. (Ephesians 4:2)

Above all, love each other deeply, because love covers over a multitude of sins. (1 Peter 4:8)

The Feeding of the Three

We've had some frosty mornings recently. And as soon as the daylight appears, dozens of birds flock into the garden outside my window to feast on the feeders and the seed that my owner's scattered around on the ground. And it's rather a shame that some of them have to let the side down. Because there's plenty of food to go around, but some still have to squabble over it. They want it all for themselves.

Which made it all the more pleasing when I heard about the following story. A couple of humans walked into a convenience store which sold a range of freshly filled submarine rolls. They weren't together, but it so happened that their lunchbreaks coincided. Sitting outside on the pavement was a homeless man. He wasn't actively begging, but he sat there with that look of tired resignation that's etched onto the faces of so many folk in his position.

The human that had gone in first thought about him as he ordered his roll. He'd worked all morning. He was hungry. But as he left, he decided to hand over his roll to the homeless man, who thanked him.

He then started to walk back to the office where he worked. He'd gone a short distance when the second human that had been behind him in the shop came running up behind him. And this human insisted on giving up half of his roll to the first one. So, in the end, no one went hungry. The generosity of the two meant that all three of them were fed.

And this made me think back to the story of 'The Feeding of The Five Thousand' (Luke 9:10–17). This is when a young boy gave up his lunch – five loaves and a couple of fish – for Jesus to convert into enough food to feed all of the five thousand people present. And once again, no one ended up going hungry. Those who donated their food still received enough back to sustain them. You could say that God and Jesus provided for them. And that's quite a thought, in a world that's so full of the 'haves' and the 'have-nots' . . . .

Give, and it will be given to you.
(Luke 6:38a).

He who gives to the poor
will lack nothing . . . .
(Proverbs 28:27a).

Remember this: Whoever sows sparingly will also reap sparingly, and whoever sows generously will also reap generously.
(2 Corinthians 9:6).

The Fright of My Life

It started off as a normal morning. It was a murky day outside. I was busy preening on a perch next to the kitchen window, and my owner was sitting at the table right next to me, eating his breakfast and listening to the radio. When, suddenly, I let out a loud shriek of panic and fell to the ground. My owner was a bit slow to react, thinking that I'd simply slipped off my perch. He casually turned to look, and then his eyes came face to face with those of a large female Sparrowhawk, sitting on the windowsill the other side of the glass. There was a look of malevolence in the Sparrowhawk's eyes, and it was clearly after having me for its breakfast. My owner leapt up and shouted. The Sparrowhawk didn't bat an eyelid, but continued its cold, steely stare. Finally, my owner rushed to the window next to where the Sparrowhawk was sitting, and flung it open, and only then did it fly away.

This was an unwelcome reminder of the daily terrors faced by the wild birds in the garden. And it was also a reminder that our world is far from perfect, especially when compared to Heaven. For in Heaven, there is no system of predator and prey; no illnesses or diseases like Covid; no natural disasters; no threat of death or loss; no accidents; no fears or worries or insecurities. Heaven offers us all the perfect warmth and comfort that can only come from pure love.

And I know that's hard to imagine when you look at it from the perspective of our present world. But God understands this. And it's because He understands our situation so well, that He gave us the gift of Jesus. Jesus came to the world to experience first-hand the threats and suffering and the trouble and the pain that afflicts humanity and all creation. And to let us know that there is something much better out there, if we can only put our trust in Him. Jesus is the 'get out of jail card' for every one of us.

114

Christmas Day is fast approaching. And if we can only understand the full significance of what it really means for us, then we should be beside ourselves with hope and joy. Because the birth of Jesus shows us that God is on our side. That He cares for us, He understands us, and that He wants to help us. Even when we don't deserve it. And the promise of Salvation is the greatest Christmas present that any of us will ever receive!

> But the angel said to them, 'Do not be afraid. I bring you good news of great joy that will be for all the people. Today in the town of David, a Saviour has been born to you' … .
> (Luke:2:10–11a)

The Fruits of Our Labours

My owner is a gardener. He likes to grow all kinds of weird and wonderful produce. This year, he built a new raised bed, and then he filled it up with over 3000 litres of compost. Finally, he planted some pumpkins and squashes in it, which he continued to feed and water all through the Summer.

His plants grew incredibly well. It wasn't long before the surface of the raised bed had disappeared below a riot of green leaves and stalks. In fact, it was such a jungle, that he didn't know what lay beneath – that is until last week when the foliage started to die back. It was then that my owner climbed up onto the bed, full of anticipation. He parted some of the leaves, and discovered that underneath, there was … – absolutely nothing! No pumpkins, no squashes – no nothing!

He'd been standing there for a few moments, feeling disappointed and cheated, when a vague hint of something orange caught the corner of his eye, some distance away in a patch of nettles. He jumped down, walked across and strode deep in the nettles, ignoring the stings he received along the way. And there, far away from where the plants had been growing in the raised bed, sat the most enormous orange pumpkin. In fact, some seven stone of pumpkin which took an almighty amount of shifting. And not only the pumpkin, but also half a dozen beautifully formed winter squashes.

And so my owner came to learn an important lesson. Because you can work and toil all through life, but you can't always see the fruits of your labours. And it's so easy for us to feel a sense of despair or frustration – or even a sense of worthlessness – when in fact all the time, we've been achieving great results. It's just that we can't always see it. It must be like that for so many schoolteachers, doctors, politicians and vicars. And it's probably like that for a great many Christians too. Think of every kind act and every good deed. Every time you stop to listen or place a coin in a charity box, you're making a difference, and helping to make the world that little bit better than it was before. Even when you're not aware of it ....

I am the true vine, and My Father is the gardener. He cuts off every branch in Me that bears no fruit, while every branch that does bear fruit He prunes so that it will be even more fruitful. (John 15:1–2)

The Living Miracle of Spring

Well, Spring has sprung, and it's a joy to be a parrot! The flowers are all unfurling outside. The birds are singing and beginning to nest. And the air is filled with both the smell and sound of humans mowing their lawns. This is my favourite time of year. All Nature feels good! There is a richness and a lushness everywhere. A sense of optimism, hope and expectation.

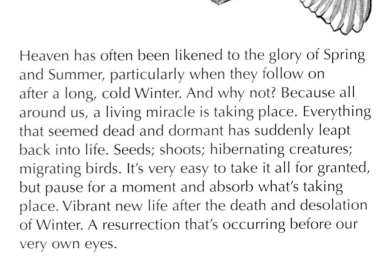

Heaven has often been likened to the glory of Spring and Summer, particularly when they follow on after a long, cold Winter. And why not? Because all around us, a living miracle is taking place. Everything that seemed dead and dormant has suddenly leapt back into life. Seeds; shoots; hibernating creatures; migrating birds. It's very easy to take it all for granted, but pause for a moment and absorb what's taking place. Vibrant new life after the death and desolation of Winter. A resurrection that's occurring before our very own eyes.

If you stop to stare at the beauty of the Spring, Heaven won't seem so far away. The reality of the resurrection, Salvation and our own afterlife all seem more plausible. And we begin to understand the message of hope that Paul writes in his letter to the Roman churches:

> I consider that our present sufferings are not worth comparing to the glory that will be revealed in us … creation itself will be liberated from its bondage to decay and brought into the glorious freedom of the children of God.   (Romans 8: 18 and 21)

Open your eyes and open your mind to the glorious miracle of Springtime. And then imagine an eternal Spring….

The 'Lonely Hearts' Column

I like to count my parrot blessings every single day. Because my adopted human family understand that I need to be at the heart of their family life. Otherwise, I could so easily feel lonely and forgotten. As it is, I know that I'm very much valued, loved and appreciated.

Not everyone is so fortunate. Many folk go through life feeling very lonely. And loneliness can be like a toothache of the soul, flaring up, and relentlessly gnawing away at us inside. And that's why some folk turn to the 'Lonely Hearts' column of various publications, in their quest to find friendship and love. Unfortunately, not everyone wants to meet up for the 'right reasons', which can make it all a bit of a minefield.

There's one particular advertisement which appeared in the *Atlanta Journal* in America which I thought I'd share with you. It went like this:

'A single black female seeks male companionship. Ethnicity not important, but would prefer a Christian male.

I'm a very good girl who LOVES to play. I'd enjoy long walks in the woods, riding in your pickup truck, camping and fishing trips, plus cozy winter nights lying by the fire. Candlelit dinners will have me eating out of your hand; afterwards I'd love snuggling up with you.

I'll be at the front door when you get home from work, wearing only what nature gave me ... .'

A bit further down the page, at the end of the advertisement, this lady included a photograph of herself. And she turned out to be a black Labrador!

The fact is, a great many humans, animals and birds need love and companionship. Without it, they are incomplete. And just like humans, a great many birds and animals form life-long bonds with one another.

God never intended us to prowl around like the lonely old bears of the northern forests. Throughout the Gospels, Jesus compares humanity to a flock of sheep, emphasising the need for togetherness. While working on the streets of Calcutta, Mother Teresa came to see this first-hand:

> The most terrible poverty is loneliness, and the feeling of being unloved.
> (Mother Teresa: 1910–1997. *Posthumously made a Saint by the Catholic Church for her missionary work in Calcutta, India*)

It's a situation that so many of us want to avoid, and which troubles us greatly:

> The trouble is not that I am single and likely to stay single, but that I am lonely and likely to stay lonely.
> (Charlotte Bronte: 1816–1855. *British novelist and poet and eldest of the three Bronte sisters*)

Every local church can play a huge role in the battle against loneliness. And they can do it by welcoming everyone that walks through the door, and by reaching out into their local communities.

I feel very blessed with my daily life, and I want others to feel the same ....

The widow who is really in need and left all alone puts her hope in God and continues night and day to pray and to ask God for help. (1 Timothy 5:5)

The Lottery of Life

You know, Life can seem like one giant lottery for both humans and parrots alike. If 'luck' is on your side, then you end up with a nice owner, or a nice home in some Amazonian tree that doesn't get chopped down by loggers. You avoid illness and accidents. You are born or hatched out in a territory where food and water are abundant. You find a loving partner who stays with you all through your life.

in the world, rather than those that are living abundantly? And why should one child become seriously ill while their sibling stays totally healthy?

When I get to Heaven, I will have so many questions to ask about the way our world operates. Especially about its apparent unfairness. The world in which Jesus walked was just as unfair as our present one. Full of 'the haves' and 'the have-nots', the healthy and the sick.

But if so-called 'luck' is against you, then all kinds of unfortunate things can occur.

Of course, we can all help to make our own 'luck' by living our lives sensibly and avoiding unnecessary risk. But that isn't the whole story. Why are some humans born into terrible poverty? Why do natural disasters usually hit the poorest humans or rarest creatures

Jesus never really explained to us why our world is like it is, but He certainly showed us how we should live out our lives to help others less fortunate than ourselves.

I have a lovely human friend who has two grandchildren – Isaac and Max. Isaac, the older brother, is bright, happy, and at the age of four, beginning to discover life. And yet he's just been diagnosed with Muscular Dystrophy. I've included a photo of him with his younger brother, Max. I guess we will never fully understand why such things happen to four-year olds and their families. And we might not be able to stop it from happening. But by following the example of Jesus, we can still pray for all of the Isaacs of this world.

The Bible says a lot about us helping one another:

Virtually all of us have the power to do something every day to help. Whether that be a simple prayer, lending a helping hand or making a charitable donation. Every day we're given the chance to do something positive for the world around us. A chance that's too precious to waste. And a chance that makes our day worthwhile. And that even applies to a simple parrot!

Carry each other's burdens, and in this way you will fulfil the law of Christ.
(Galatians 6:2)

Do not withhold good from those deserve it, when it is in your power to act.   Proverbs (3:27)

And do not forget to do good and to share with others … . (Hebrews 13:16)

Each of you should not look only to your own interests, but also to the interests of others.   (Philippians 2:4)

Share with God's people who are in need … .   (Romans 12:13a)

The Magpie and the Wren

I love sitting by the window and watching all of the activity around the bird feeders in the garden. The action is a bit like a microcosm of life.

At the top end of the 'pecking order' are the Magpies. They are smart and powerful, walking with a distinctive swagger. They exude self-importance, and they are usually linked to any trouble taking place in the garden. You could describe them as the 'self-made mega bosses of the bird world' enjoying all the trimmings of life, often at the expense of others. A great many birds visit the garden every day, with the majority of them paying due homage to the Magpies.

But at the other end of the spectrum – at the very bottom of the pile, come the tiny Wrens. They are small, drab and insignificant, quietly going about their business. Blink and you miss them. And yet, these tiny creatures have a gift which outshines all of the other birds in the garden. And that's their voice. A voice that's not only beautiful and melodious, but also miraculous. If you measure the song of a wren in relation to its body weight, then it is ten times louder than the crowing of a cockerel. And it's also incredibly intricate. Wrens produce between 16 and 36 notes per second, many of which are inaudible to the human ear. All from a tiny bird weighing just seven to twelve grams. You would need some 1400 Wrens to match the body weight of an average Mute Swan.

There are days when we can easily feel a bit down. In fact, downtrodden, unappreciated and unnoticed. Overshadowed by those who are bigger, louder or more aggressive than ourselves. But what really lurks inside us? Because we've all been given something by God to develop and to use and to nurture. Just like the insignificant Wren. And the Bible reminds us of just that.

There's no pecking order in Heaven. Everyone is unique and special and equally valued. And if we all use the gifts we've been given for God's purpose, then we can move mountains. We can change the world. That's quite a thought, isn't it?

So, from now on, I'm going to stop looking in the mirror and thinking how beautiful my feathers are. Because true beauty isn't just what you can see on the outside. God's special gifts to all of us are often hidden within. Sitting quietly inside us, waiting to be discovered and then offered to the world . . . .

> We have different gifts, according to the grace given us.
> (Romans 12:6a)
>
> But each man has his own gift from God; one has this gift, another has that.
> (1 Corinthians 7:7b)

The Meaning of Lent

The Easter weekend will soon be with us, and humans find themselves in the midst of that special time called Lent. And 'Lent' is one of those strange human names because it sounds as though you've given something to somebody with the expectation of getting it back. But it's not only parrots that find Lent confusing as the following story shows....

An Irishman moved into a small village, and immediately went along to the local pub. He walked in and ordered three beers all at once. The bartender raised his eyebrows, but served the man as requested, and watched as the man sat quietly at a table on his own, drinking the beers one after another.

An hour later, the Irishman ordered three more. And for the following few nights, this became the established pattern. Soon most of the village were whispering about 'the man who always ordered three pints.'

Finally, after a week had passed, the bartender broached the subject on behalf of the village. 'I don't mean to pry, but folks around here are wondering why you always order three pints at a time?' 'Tis odd, isn't it?' replied the Irishman. 'You see, I have two brothers. One emigrated to America and the other to Australia. We promised each other that we would always order an extra two beers whenever we drank as a way of keeping up the family bond.'

The bartender and the rest of the village liked this answer and warmed to the Irishman. But then, one day, he came in and only ordered two beers. The bartender poured them with a heavy heart, and this was repeated later on in the evening and the following day. Before long, prayers were being said for the Irishman. Eventually, the bartender said to him: 'Folks around here including myself, want to offer their condolences to you for the death of one of your brothers; you know, the two beers instead of three.' To which the Irishman replied: 'Nobody's died. I decided to give up drinking for Lent.'

So the Irishman did, but didn't really give up his beer for Lent. And around the world right now, many humans will be going without special treats like chocolate or cakes or a glass of wine in recognition of Jesus' sacrifice on the cross. But you know, 'giving up' doesn't always mean going without. Because giving up can also mean 'getting rid of'. Getting rid of those things which can so often separate us from God. Things like guilt and regret. Or addictions like gambling or drug taking. Or unresolved conflict or anger. These things are much bigger than beer or chocolate or cakes, and if we can only manage to resolve them or expel them during this time of Lent, there will be much rejoicing in Heaven. And Jesus' sacrifice on the cross will become all the more relevant to our lives.

Do not conform any longer to the pattern of this world, but be transformed by the renewing of your mind. Then you will be able to test and approve what God's will is .... (Romans 12:2a)

The Miracle That's Us!

My owner recently had one of those ancestry DNA tests done to find out about his origins. And the results were very interesting. He turned out to be mainly English, but he also had some Spanish, Eastern European, Irish, French, and Belgian blood in his system. And perhaps most interesting of all, he turned out to be 5% Viking. So what do these results really say about him? Well, probably not a great deal because most humans have a hotchpotch of ancestral threads in their make-up. It's a bit different for me. As a Senegal Parrot, I guess that my DNA is 100% Senegalese!

The very fact that we're here at all is nothing short of a miracle. Because throughout the centuries, so many ancestral chains have been abruptly severed because of sickness, plagues and wars. Because of drought, famine and infertility. And because of tragedy, accidents, and a lack of medical knowledge and care. And then, what about the challenges posed by climatic changes, freak weather conditions, perilous migrations or dangerous animals and dinosaurs? By rights, hardly any of us should be here. We shouldn't have had the chance to be hatched or born. And yet somehow we exist! And every one of us that is alive today has literally won the world's greatest lottery! Even if you think you're having a terrible day! It would take a very gifted statistician to work out the odds of us ever getting this far.

And even as a small, humble parrot, I never want to take for granted the miracle of my life! The miracle of my existence. The opportunity I've been given to develop, to grow and to become the unique and remarkable creature that I am. We've all been given a very precious chance to make our mark and to do something good for the world!

Every single day, we're reminded of the brevity and fragility of our worldly lives through the passing of our loved ones, by stories in the media and through the deterioration of our own health. So every living day is an opportunity to be grabbed for all it's worth! Because we're all surfing on the crest of a miracle. Which leads me to ask this question. Is the miracle of our existence simply a statistical fluke? Or is it more than that?

And whatever you do, whether in word or deed, do it all in the name of the Lord Jesus, giving thanks to God the Father through him.

(Colossians 3:17)

Be joyful always; pray continually; give thanks in all circumstances, for this is God's will for you in Jesus Christ.

(1Thessalonians 5:16–18)

Have we been given our place on Earth as part of some extraordinary master plan? That's a question that every one of us needs to ask as we live out our lives. For if you come to the conclusion that a loving Creator placed you here, it will affect who you are and everything you do for the rest of your worldly life ….

The Paradox of Eastertime

I've been sitting here on my perch this morning practicing 'Advanced Cerebral Parrot Yoga.' Because the more I sit and think about God, this world, and my overall place in it, the more I seem to tie my brain up in knots. The more I discover about Christianity, the more my parrot logic gets turned on its head.

Just think about the Christian life. Jesus tells us that we need to give if we are to receive. In order to see, we must accept that we're blind. To discover true wisdom, we must reduce ourselves down to the level of small children. Quite often, we have to suffer in order to gain. And then, for our grand finale, we all need to die in order to truly live.

The Bible tells us that the first will be last and that the last will be first. Jesus, the Son of God, reduces Himself down to the level of basic humanity, and instead of saving Himself from the ordeal of the cross, He chooses to suffer to save a world of lesser beings. And here's the real crux. *Yes, Jesus would rather die in agony on the cross than exist in Heaven without us. Because His love for each one of us, warts and all, is so immeasurably great….*

I may be a simple parrot, but I find this all mind-boggling.
Overwhelming.
Disconcerting.
Even stupefying.
And at this Eastertime, it shows me that the power of God's love for us all, is more powerful than anything else we will ever know or experience . . . .

For God so loved the world that he gave his one and only Son that whoever believes in him shall not perish but have eternal life.   (John 3:16)

Therefore, if anyone is in Christ, he is a new creation; the old has gone, the new has come!   (2 Corinthians 5:17)

For whoever wants to save his life will lose it, but whoever loses his life for me will save it.   (Luke 9:24)

Now if we died with Christ, we believe that we will also live with him.   (Romans 6:8)

So the last will be first, and the first will be last.   (Matthew 20:16)

The Parrot Valentino

Valentine's Day is getting close. And did you know that parrots can also have special valentines? Here's my story....

In a nearby village, there lives a lady Vicar called Penny. Every time I meet her, my eyeballs dilate and my quills start to rattle. It's always been love at first sight between us. She whispers sweet nothings into my ears, and in return, I fluff up my feathers and offer to regurgitate. Sometimes several weeks pass when we don't see each other, but that makes every subsequent meeting all the more precious. And although Penny has a human husband in tow, I've become her feathery admirer. And for the last couple of years, I've sent her a special Valentine's Card. It's made up from my finest feathers that fall out during the preceding year.

And the reason why I love Penny is probably because I sense so much of God inside her. After all, God is real love and God is pure love. When you're drawn to someone because you sense so much goodness inside them, you're

really responding to the presence of
God inside them. And it's my heartfelt
wish that you can also share Valentine's
Day with someone who radiates pure
love from their soul ... .

Love is patient, love is kind. It does not envy, it does
not boast, it is not proud. It is not rude, it is not self-
seeking, it is not easily angered, it keeps no record of
wrongs. Love does not delight in evil but rejoices with
the truth. It always protects, always trusts, always
hopes, and always perseveres.   (1Corinthians 13: 4–7)

God is love. Whoever lives in love lives in God, and
God in him.   (1John: 4:16b)

When the power of love overcomes the love of power,
the world will know peace.   (Jimi Hendrix)

The Power of Positive Thinking

I've noticed how you can divide humans up into two separate sub-species. There are the ones that exist with their glass half full, and those for whom it's always half empty. The optimists and the pessimists. Optimistic humans live out their lives with a certain amount of idealism. A belief that things will eventually turn out okay, even when there appears to be no light at the end of the tunnel. Meanwhile, pessimists prefer to gaze upon the stark reality of the present. Towards all of the things that are not right, and unlikely ever to improve.

So where do Christians fit in with all this? Well, Christians believe in God and Jesus and the Holy Spirit. They believe in an underlying purpose and end goal for their existence here on Earth. They believe that Jesus is their Saviour, and that they are destined for eternal life in Heaven. So they are definitely 'glass half full' optimists. Pessimists can argue that Christian belief is a form of 'pie in the sky' idealism. But there's a problem with this type of mindset. Because it can easily develop into a self-fulfilling prophecy. For if you've got no desire to improve your own life, or the lives of others around you, then nothing will ever change.

One of the shining inspirational figures of the Coronavirus pandemic has been Captain Sir Tom Moore. He proved that idealistic dreams can become reality. Yes, there was Captain Tom – a diminutive 100 year old war veteran, disabled and only able to walk with the aid of a metal frame. And yet he was able to walk far enough with that frame to raise nearly £33 million for the NHS before finally falling victim to Covid. He made the impossible come true through positive thinking.

If I have learned one thing from all that has happened it's that it is never too late to start something new and make a difference, especially if it brings light and life to people around the world. There is a future for everyone and there is always room for a global expansion in kindness.
(Captain Sir Tom Moore: London 2020: Penguin Michael Joseph: *Tomorrow will be a Good Day*: pp 371–2).

Now, I don't know whether Captain Tom had any Christian beliefs or not, but his faith and self-belief in what can be achieved against the odds mirrors the same belief that many Christians have in God and Jesus. The belief that there is something much bigger and better out there just waiting to be discovered or achieved. Irrespective of our age or who we are or what we may have done in the past. And it was this same kind of belief and realisation that enabled sinners in the Bible to change their lives around and to start to trust in Jesus. For example, when Jesus was anointed by the sinful woman at the house of Simon the Pharisee. The woman had a sudden moment of reckoning, turning away from her negative past to embrace the positivity of a new life with Jesus.

> Therefore I tell you, her many sins have been forgiven – for she loved much.
> (Luke 7:47)

We all need to ditch the negativity of pessimism for it does nothing but restrict us. Christianity is all about stepping out from the shadow of pessimism to embrace optimism. Only then can we achieve our full potential … .

> The positive thinker sees the invisible, feels the intangible, and achieves the impossible.
> (Winston Churchill: 1874–1965. *UK Prime Minister 1939–45; 1951–55*)

> The greatest discovery of all time is that a person can change his future by merely changing his attitude.
> (Oprah Winfrey: 1954–present. *US Talk show host and philanthropist*)

> Do not conform any longer to the pattern of this world, but be transformed by the renewing of your mind.
> (Romans 12:2)

The Power Within Us

Parrots are well known for being brightly coloured. There are a few exceptions to the rule, but on the whole, we add a touch of brightness to the world. Just looking at us can cheer people up! Reds, yellows, greens, blues – often strikingly combined. You could call us an extravagant expression of well-being and hope. So our mere appearance helps us to make a positive impact on the world around us.

Of course, humans don't have colourful feathers. They just come in various shades of brown, white and yellow. So if they want to make a visual impact, I guess they have to dye their hair some outlandish colour.

Or is that really true?

Is it really your appearance that counts, or is it what lies beneath that interests God? Because humans can have the plainest of faces, or the most boringly coloured hair, but if they choose to, they can still project a sense of warmth and well-being, comfort and goodness, upon the world around them. Through their eyes. Through their smiles. And through a whole multitude of other facial expressions. And this is where humans have the advantage over parrots. Our beaks only go up and down. You can't smile with a beak. Our feathers hide our facial expressions. And although our eyes can twinkle, because they're set on the side of our heads, we lose the dual impact of them looking at somebody full in the face.

So this means that humans have been given the chance to subtly impact the world around them. To set 'the feel' and 'the tone' amongst those that they come into contact with. And it's totally down to each individual as to the kind of impact that they choose to make. Do they send out messages of love or hate? Of warmth or coldness? Of understanding or indifference? Of togetherness or separation?

Kindness makes you the most beautiful person in the world no matter what you look like.

A human face can paint a thousand different pictures. A single expression can be the difference between love and discord or war and peace. So as you go about your business today, what colours are you painting the world around you? Are you making it a happier place or a worse place to be? Are you making people feel better, or are you causing them to shy away? And most importantly of all – are you helping to project God's love upon the face of the Earth? Because if all humanity did that each day, this world would change for ever.

You are the light of the world … let your light shine before men … . (Matthew 5:14–16)

The Question of Gifts

Do you think I could be described as 'a gifted parrot'? After all, it's not every parrot that can write and publish a book. Or discern so much about Life, the world and our relationship with God while sitting on an old, wizened perch. So does that make me gifted?

'Oh dear' I hear you say. 'Fame is starting to go to that bird's head!' But it's not really like that. Because I believe we are all gifted. God has created every one of us as a unique individual, all with our own set of special gifts, qualities and abilities. And half the battle is discovering who we really are, what we're good at, and then fulfilling that newly discovered potential.

Quite often, we can see the special gifts in others around us, long before we recognize our own. So as Christians, we need to be beacons of encouragement, empowering one other to achieve our full potential. Not just for ourselves, but more importantly for God. And there's lots written about this in the Bible.

We all have so much to offer. Like seeds waiting to germinate; buds waiting to flower; eggs waiting to hatch .... But this isn't simply about ourselves. It's about our potential to help others. To serve God. To do good. And to make this world a better place for everyone.

The American author, Leo Buscaglia once said:

> Your talent is God's gift to you. What you do with it is your gift back to God.
>
> (Leo Buscaglia: 1924–1998. *American author, motivational speaker and academic professor*)

So folks, a parrot I may be. And a small one at that. But I'm going to carry on with my writing for the sake of parrots, humanity and God!

> Every good and perfect gift is from above, coming down from the Father … . (James 1:17a)
>
> We have different gifts, according to the grace given to us. If a man's gift is prophesying, let him use it … . If it is serving, let him serve; if it is teaching, let him teach; if it is encouraging, let him encourage; if it is contributing to the needs of others, let him give generously; if it is leadership, let him govern diligently … .
>
> (Romans 12: 6–8a)
>
> Each one (of you) should use whatever gift he has received to serve others … . (1 Peter 4:10a)

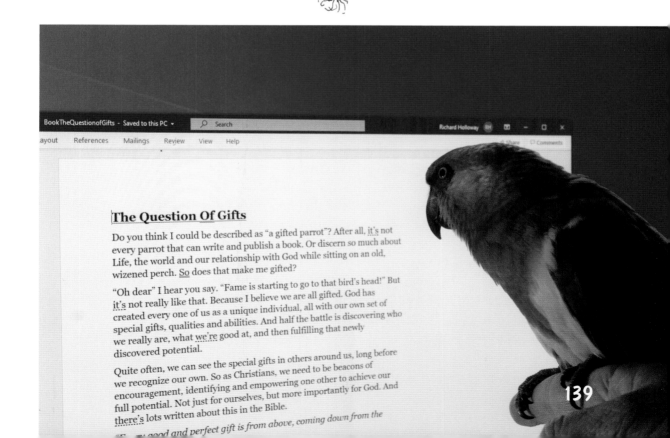

The Question Of Gifts

Do you think I could be described as "a gifted parrot"? After all, it's not every parrot that can write and publish a book. Or discern so much about Life, the world and our relationship with God while sitting on an old, wizened perch. So does that make me gifted?

"Oh dear" I hear you say. "Fame is starting to go to that bird's head!" But it's not really like that. Because I believe we are all gifted. God has created every one of us as a unique individual, all with our own set of special gifts, qualities and abilities. And half the battle is discovering who we really are, what we're good at, and then fulfilling that newly discovered potential.

Quite often, we can see the special gifts in others around us, long before we recognize our own. So as Christians, we need to be beacons of encouragement, identifying and empowering one other to achieve our full potential. Not just for ourselves, but more importantly for God. And there's lots written about this in the Bible.

"Every good and perfect gift is from above, coming down from the

139

The Sheep that Went Over the Edge of the Cliff

I live in quite a rural area, not far from the sea. In some parts, there are wild, rugged fields grazed by sheep which run right up to the edge of the sea, or in some cases, sea cliffs. I heard this story the other day, and thought I'd share it with you.

A careless sheep went too close to the edge of a local cliff, and slipped over. It finished up stuck on a narrow ledge some twenty-five feet down. The farmer was alerted, but did nothing, He simply carried on with his other duties. In fact, the sheep lay there for three whole days and nights before the farmer eventually abseiled down the cliff to rescue it. By this time, it had become very weak and exhausted. As the farmer brought the sheep safely back to the top of the cliff, a passer-by came along and criticized him for not reacting sooner. But the farmer calmly replied that had he attempted the rescue any sooner, the sheep would probably have jumped to its death. He had to wait for it to become tired and lacklustre in order to rescue it successfully.

Sometimes in our own lives, we can find ourselves imploring God to help us, yet nothing seems to happen. But, like that sheep, and the passer-by, we don't understand the full picture. God always works in God's time. He will help us when the time is right, or if it is in our best interests to do so. And we simply have to hand our problems over to Him with an open, trusting heart. The Bible tells us this, time and time again . . . .

Real trust – especially trust in adversity – is a rare and priceless virtue that will make God love us even more . . . .

Trust in the Lord and do good . . . .
(Psalm 37:3)

Trust in the Lord with all your heart . . . .
(Proverbs 3:5)

Trust in the Lord for ever . . . .
(Isaiah 26:4)

Do not let your hearts be troubled. Trust in God; trust also in Me . . . .
(John 14:1)

I will put my trust in Him . . . .
(Hebrews 2:13)

The Tree of Life

I love going up to my owner's bedroom, because from there I get a wonderful view of our village and the countryside all around. And while I'm strutting my stuff up and down on the window sill, there's one very large Beech Tree which always catches my eye. At this time of year, it looks like 'an upside-down tree' because it doesn't have any leaves. But come the Spring and the Summer, it's seemingly dead branches explode into a glorious green canopy.

I often wonder how many leaves there are on that tree. They must number at least 80,000 by the time we get to the

month of May. For by then, the tree is an absolute picture of green vibrancy. An extraordinary statement of new life, new beginnings, and new hope. And it's all quite hard to believe when I look out at that tree on a cold, wet January morning.

And you know, humans are a bit like the leaves on that tree. Because mathematicians tells us that in the UK, an average human is likely to meet over 80,000 different people during their lifetime. That's more than enough to fill the Olympic Stadium in London.

Every year, my owner sends out lots of Christmas cards and a Christmas circular to some of those people that he's decided to stay in touch with. Old friends, neighbours, work colleagues, holiday acquaintances – there are a great many of them. And sadly, at this time of year – post Christmas – he receives letters back saying that some of these folk passed away earlier in the year.

Thinking back to the Beech Tree, I know that every green leaf on that tree will eventually turn brown, shrivel and finally fall off. And if that's how it were all to end, then Life would indeed be so very sad. But it doesn't end like that. The branches may seem cold, stark and bare right now, but beneath the surface, new life is waiting to emerge. And that's how it will be for my owner and for so many

of the friends and acquaintances that he has made throughout his lifetime. This extraordinary Beech Tree is a living symbol of the promise of life that awaits us all after our apparent death. We're all part of a process, a cycle, and a pattern crafted by God. And like the leaves on that tree, so many of us will re-emerge once more, fresh, new, vibrant – and totally alive!

And the Lord God made all kinds of trees grow out of the ground – trees that were pleasing to the eye and good for food. In the middle of the garden were the tree of life and the tree of knowledge .... (Genesis 2:9a)

Jesus said to her: 'I am the resurrection and the life. He who believes in Me will live even though he dies ....'
(John 11:25)

The Will to Survive and the Grace to Receive

Many of us like to have places where we feel warm and safe. Somewhere we can retreat to in the knowledge that we are sheltered from the elements and tucked away from danger. Humans have their houses, their 'man caves' and that other little place they call 'the loo.' Other creatures have holes or burrows or nooks and crannies. And I have my favourite spot on the clothes airer, hidden amongst the rows of human plumage, all hanging up to dry. No passing hawk would ever find me there!

The will to survive is very much etched into our DNA. Irrespective of who we are, and whatever may have happened to us in the past. We all need our place of retreat. Even when we own nothing and have nowhere to go. And that's why homeless humans often take refuge in subways, underpasses and doorways. None of these places offer great shelter, but they are better than nothing.

And I recently heard about one such human that had set up home inside a local bus shelter. It kept the rain off his head, and the worst of the wind at bay. In fact, during the run-up to Christmas, this human even adorned the shelter with a set of fairy lights to make it feel more homely.

But a situation like this can cause some difficulties. Because bus passengers could no longer use the bus shelter as originally intended. And humans can be very wary of homeless people. I mean, why are they homeless in the first place? Is it drink or drugs? A violent temper or mental health issues? And do they pose a threat? It can all be a bit of a minefield. So as a fellow human, should you object to their presence, quietly ignore them, or do 'the Jesus thing' and try to help them? Sometimes prayer can supply us with the answer.

In the case of the human in the bus shelter, a few folk were touched by his plight, and they did help. They made sure he received a hot 'ready meal' every day. And when it was his birthday, they supplied a cake and a birthday card which made him cry. He cried because it was an act of love which touched him deep inside. Maybe it was the first card he'd received in years. Whatever, these small acts of kindness prevented him from becoming totally isolated from the rest of humanity.

This man was probably no angel. He'd made some serious mistakes along the way. But these few kind people were giving him a way back. An opportunity to reconnect with society instead of staying as an outcast.

And that's what God and Jesus are all about. Because just like this man, we are also 'sinful outcasts.' And as sinners, we don't always deserve a way back into the fold. Irrespective of whether we live inside a bus shelter, a palace or a bird cage. But God and Jesus don't walk on by. They don't ignore us. Instead of leaving us lost, they offer us Salvation and redemption.

Because they know that compassion, kindness, thoughtfulness and love are really at the root of what we need. And if we can offer it to others, without putting ourselves in danger, then we are fulfilling the work of God and Jesus here on Earth. Which is why Jesus told us all to:

Love your neighbour as yourself.
(Matthew 22:39b).

After a difficult few months of living rough, it seems that this human is poised to return home. To the place where he once lived a great many miles away. And there, he will hopefully get a permanent roof over his head, and the support of others, as he begins another new chapter in his eventful life.

The Wind in My Feathers

When the weather's nice, (and when the local Sparrowhawk isn't doing its rounds), I sometimes go out into the garden for a treat. I love to feel the breeze ruffling up my feathers, and I like to imagine that I'm feeling the Holy Spirit flowing through me.
And I'm mindful of what the writer Corrie ten Boom once wrote. She said:

> Faith sees the invisible, believes the unbelievable, and receives the impossible.
> (Corrie ten Boom: 1892–1983. *Christian author and survivor of a Nazi concentration camp*)

Of course, you can't see, hear or touch the Holy Spirit. But if you can open up your heart and let the Holy Spirit flow through you, then you will know when you've been touched inside. Maybe after days of prayer, you'll wake up one morning with an unequivocal answer to your problem. Or maybe you'll suddenly feel able to do something that once seemed impossible. Such as saying sorry, or forgiving someone. It's very hard for living creatures to comprehend the Holy Spirit. But, in a parrot's nutshell, if we allow the Holy Spirit to enter us, then we're allowing the will and the essence of God to come inside us too. And it can help us to change and to grow. So that we become equipped with a new inner strength. A sudden 'knowing'. Fresh wisdom. A purpose. A role. A direction. And most important of all, an opportunity to serve God.

I'm sure that the Holy Spirit touched me deep inside when I decided to write this book. After all, how many parrots go ahead and do that sort of thing? And the Holy Spirit was present at the conception,

the baptism and the temptation of Jesus here on Earth. And the Holy Spirit gave strength, focus and direction to the disciples as they ventured out into the world to spread the Christian message.

There are times when we can all be a bit stubborn or shut-off. (Even parrots!) I wonder how many times the Holy Spirit has tried to enter us, only to remain blocked off? When our inner door's been slammed shut and locked? And that can sometimes happen because of our pride or our narrowness, or because we like to believe that we're totally self-sufficient. But this can result in a lot of needless suffering, and our failure to fulfil our full potential.

Jesus knew that our lives are shaped by what we store up inside:

> The good man brings good things out of the good stored up in his heart, and the evil man brings evil things out of the evil stored up in his heart. (Luke 6:45a).

So maybe today can be a special day. The day when we allow the Holy Spirit inside us to fill our hearts with goodness and love. To allow us to become bigger, stronger, wiser and purer than we ever thought possible … .

The Wisdom to Know What I Can and Cannot Do

As parrots go, I'm a bit of a thinker, an observer and a philosopher. And as I sit here on my perch, looking out at the world beyond, I also wish I could be a reformer. A catalyst for change. A dynamic force so that I can somehow make right what I believe to be wrong with the world around me.

Of course, the world isn't all bad. I see a lot of goodness and kindness going on all around. But I also see too much injustice, unfairness, cruelty and self-interest. There are days when I simply want to wave a magic wand and make it all right. So that we no longer have a world full of 'haves' and 'have-nots'; a world obsessed with money instead of moral and spiritual values; a world that's focussed on worldly status instead of our status before God; and a world in which creation is disrespected and destroyed, instead of being valued, treasured and revered.

There is so much that I see around that I simply can't change. Because I'm only one small parrot in the midst of a mighty machine called humanity. And there are some days when this could easily make me feel helpless and insignificant. Or sad and depressed. But that's when I turn to a famous old prayer written by Reinhold Niebuhr. Because it could easily have been written just for me ....

God,
Grant me the serenity
To accept the things I cannot change;
Courage to change the things I can;
And wisdom to know the difference.
Living one day at a time;
Enjoying one moment at a time.
Accepting hardships as a pathway to peace;
Taking as He did, this sinful world
As it is, not as I would have it;
Trusting that He will make all things right
If I surrender to Your will;
So that I may be reasonably happy in this life
And supremely happy with You forever in the next.
Amen

(Reinhold Niebuhr: 1892–1971.
American author and theologian, and author of the
'Serenity Prayer')

Progress has little to do with speed, but much to do with direction

No, I can't change the ways of the world. But what I can do is put my faith in God. Many human beings will continue to spoil life for one another, and to annihilate the world around them. Unfortunately, not all of them are bright enough to see what they are doing.

But I also know this. That the next world is going to be so very, very different. And it will seem all the more wonderful for the very fact that I experienced life here first.

This World's Not Heaven

I spend a lot of my day positioned next to a large kitchen window. I love looking out over the lush green lawn and colourful flowerbeds, and I particularly like watching the wild birds. My owner attracts them into the garden with feeders containing sunflower hearts, suet, dried mealworms and seed. All kinds of birds visit us, including finches, sparrows, thrushes, woodpeckers, nuthatches, wrens, tits and pigeons. They all have their own character, style and personality. And they're lovely to watch. There's even a chubby Bank Vole that counts as one of 'the regular diners'.

However, not all of the visitors are welcome. There's always someone that has to spoil the party. And in our case, it's the local Sparrowhawk that swoops in low over the hedge and seizes any slow or unsuspecting bird. It represents the cruel, brutal side of Nature, which seems at odds with the beauty and perfection of our natural world. And because of this one villain, all of the birds in the garden live on the edge of their nerves. Ready to take flight at the slightest sound or sudden movement. It can't be much fun for them.

And not surprisingly, this leads me to ask some questions. Because the miracle of life hasn't happened by chance. It's all too intricate and detailed for that. So if we've all been made by a loving Creator, where does the concept of predator and prey fit in? Or let's take this further. What about illness and disease? Natural disasters? Pain, suffering and bereavement? How can a loving Creator allow all this to happen?

And yet, despite all of this, I along with so many others, do believe in God. When Jesus died on the cross, He probably only had a few hundred followers. Today there are almost 3 billion people (representing more than one third of the world's population) that describe themselves as Christians. And that's just humans, let alone the parrots! And it's a figure that continues to grow. How can that be?

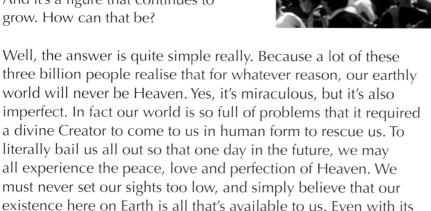

Well, the answer is quite simple really. Because a lot of these three billion people realise that for whatever reason, our earthly world will never be Heaven. Yes, it's miraculous, but it's also imperfect. In fact our world is so full of problems that it required a divine Creator to come to us in human form to rescue us. To literally bail us all out so that one day in the future, we may all experience the peace, love and perfection of Heaven. We must never set our sights too low, and simply believe that our existence here on Earth is all that's available to us. Even with its faults and imperfections, our world is far too miraculous for that.

God is not abandoning us here on Earth whenever threats, illness, disasters and suffering came our way. Instead, 'a room' is being prepared for us in Heaven. Our present lives are simply just a stepping stone along the way, as Jesus reminded His disciples....

Do not let your hearts be troubled. Trust in God; trust also in Me. In My Father's house are many rooms; if it were not so, I would have told you. I am going there to prepare a place for you.   (John 14: 1–2)

Too Hot to Handle?

People are often surprised to hear that my favourite food is chillies. Or to be more precise, the seeds from inside chillies. Unlike mammals, most birds are immune to the heat and effects of chilli seeds. This means I can have great fun! If visitors come to our house, I'll deliberately try to kiss them on the lips knowing full well that I'm passing on some residue from my beak. Then all I need to do is count to ten and wait for their reaction. It never fails! The hotter the chilli, the better the result!

And if you have a problem with squirrels or other animals eating your wild bird food, all you have to do is mix it with some chilli powder. It works a treat!

Now humans often want to push the boundaries of common sense, and try things that aren't very good for them. At our Summer village fete, there's always a chilli eating competition. Contestants have to eat a total of ten different chillies. The first one is fairly mild. But by the time they get to numbers eight, nine and ten, the heat is approaching atom bomb proportions! The eventual 'winner' normally staggers away at the end, bent-over double, with sweat and tears cascading off their face. So why do they do it?

From a parrot's perspective, humans can be very hard to understand. They all know about things that can do them great harm. Such as taking illegal drugs, excessive drinking, sniffing aerosol cans or smoking everything from weed to tobacco. And yet all around the world, millions upon millions of humans do these things every single day. Others dabble with the occult, or drive recklessly, or eat unhealthy kinds of food. So why do so many humans do it? Is it all about daring to dare, or the thrill of flirting with danger? Or simply running blind without thinking about the consequences? You could say that lemmings like to flirt with danger every time they jump over the edge of a cliff, but not too many of them crawl away afterwards.

Some things in this world can be too hot for humans to handle. When dare and bravado take over from common sense, disaster is likely to follow. And of course, disaster causes untold grief and suffering for families, friends and all kinds of other folk.

God didn't create us to be reckless and self-centred. And yet humans have a track-record of it. The greatest historical act of human recklessness was the murder of Jesus Christ upon the cross. Humans seem compelled to flirt with acts of self-destruction .... But it doesn't have to be like this. God created us to learn, to grow, to evolve and to change. To become wiser with age. To become less obsessed with the physical things in life, and more pre-occupied with the spiritual. Because it's spiritual growth that will ultimately bring us inner peace and lead us to Heaven. It's just as the Apostle Paul writes in his first letter to the Corinthians:

> The man without the Spirit does not accept the things that come from the Spirit of God, for they are foolishness to him, and he cannot understand them ....
> (1 Corinthians: 2:14).

So, do you feel God's spirit now, deep inside your being? Or are you still stuffing in the red-hot chillies, to get 'your daily fix'?

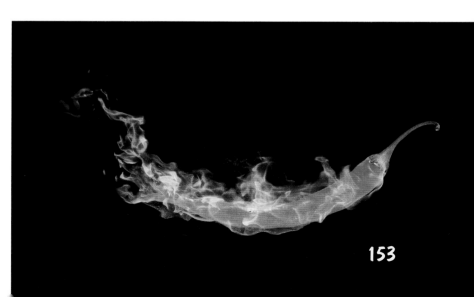

Visiting Eileen

Every morning, before breakfast, I make a short journey. I fly from one side of our house to the annexe on the other side to visit 94-year-old Eileen. Eileen is the grandma of our collective residence. These days she's a bit frail and wobbly on her legs, and she's become rather forgetful. You could say that she's no longer quite as dynamic as she once was, and it would be very easy to simply forget about her, and to focus on everything else in life. After all, I've got my preening, eating and writing to attend to. But, as I've discovered, it's very important for both of us to make time for one another. Because Eileen, despite her limitations, still shines with love. Love towards me, and love towards others. And I love her back, big time. She talks to me softly and strokes my feathers. And in return, I wolf-whistle at her, run through my repertoire of intimate sounds, and even go through the motions of regurgitation. And she always beams from ear to ear. After all, how many 94 year-olds can truthfully say that they get wolf-whistled at every morning before breakfast?

There are lots of humans around us in the world who, at first glance, don't always come across as being the most lively or dynamic of folk, but you know, they usually have something special to offer us. And that might be love, or wisdom, some encouragement, or a kind thought or prayer when we need it most. And they really appreciate us spending a little time with them. I'm not just thinking of older humans here, but folk who are sick, those with disabilities and those with conditions such as Down's Syndrome. It's often these people that end up giving us the most back if we take the time and trouble to see them. It's a two-way process.

There is one verse in the New Testament that is repeated word for word in five different books. And what it says is this:

Love your neighbour as yourself.
(Matthew 19:19; Mark 12:31; Luke 10:29; Romans 13:9; Galatians 5:14)

The problem in today's world is that humans are all so very busy. And stepping out of that 'busyness' to seize a precious moment of time can prove quite difficult. But what's more important: the bustle of a daily routine or a special moment of love and thoughtfulness shared with somebody else? I've been visiting Eileen for over ten years now. She's my neighbour in more ways than one. And what we offer to one another is something very unexpected and something very special. And we wouldn't have it any other way … .

Therefore, as we have opportunity, let us do good to all people … . (Galatians 6:10a)

Therefore encourage one another and build one another up, just as you are doing.
(1 Thessalonians 5:11)

And do not forget to do good and to share what you have with others … .
(Hebrews 13:16a)

When the Ground Opens Up

It's a beautiful sunny day outside my window. The garden is full of bright flowers. The bees are buzzing and the Summer swallows are streaking across the sky overhead. Everything looks and seems wonderful. And yet, despite all this, I know that some special human friends are suffering today because they find themselves in a time of crisis.

During our Christian journeys, we'll all face times of crisis. Unexpected troubles which test our faith to its very core. For some humans, it might be redundancy, financial worries, a bereavement or a medical crisis. And whenever a crisis comes along, irrespective of whether we have a faith or not, we can feel very alone. And many will ask the question: 'Where is God when I need Him most?'

We all want our lives to run smoothly. We don't want times of crisis. Is there ever any good to be found in suffering? Well, the famous human songwriter Leonard Cohen, believed that there was, and he wrote this very meaningful lyric in his song 'Anthem:'

Sometimes the crack can seem more like a gaping chasm with no available bridge to span the gap. That's how it must seem right now for my human friends, David and Clare. David underwent major brain surgery last week. All was going so well. He was discharged from hospital on Friday. Everything looked good until Sunday morning, when he developed a terrible headache. As the day progressed, his conditioned worsened, and he is now back in hospital in a High Dependency Unit with a suspected bleed on the brain. No one knows how things will turn out. His wife, Clare, is only allowed to spend a limited amount of time with him each day. Suddenly, a vast chasm has opened up in their lives, with dark menacing clouds hovering overhead.

There is a crack, a crack in everything that's how the light gets in.
(Leonard Cohen: 1934–2016.
Canadian singer–songwriter: verse taken from his song 'Anthem')

At times like this, Christians and non-Christians alike find themselves asking why – if there really is a God out there – He can't simply step into the chasm and make all things well again. And do it straight away.

Sudden, unexplained cures do sometimes occur. But they're not very common. Certainly not since Jesus left this world. So this leaves the onus *upon us* to step forwards into the gap. To take a real step of faith. To move forwards into a new position. To accept what is happening instead of fighting against it, allowing the light of God to radiate down upon us. Because it's at times like this that we grow as people, both mentally and spiritually. And it's in a time of crisis that so many of us will come closer to God. And that's what poor Clare is having to do right now along with many others around the world.

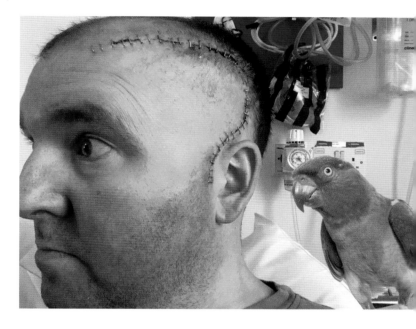

> God is our refuge and strength, an ever-present help in trouble. Therefore we will not fear, though the earth give way and the mountains fall into the heart of the sea ….
>
> (Psalm 46:1–2)

Step forwards into the chasm where the Lord is waiting for you:

> Come to me, all of you who are tired from carrying your heavy loads, and I will give you rest …. (Matthew11:28

Step forwards so His light can shine down upon you ….

Postscript:
In the end, David was able to leave hospital without requiring any further surgery. However, he sadly lost his fight for life shortly before this book was published

Who Is My Neighbour?

I have a very good human friend called Penny Lawson. She's a local Vicar, and in fact we're such good friends that I've been known to share my special parrot treats with her. (And yes, she enjoyed them!)

A few days ago, Penny told me a moving story which I'd like to share with you. She'd gone shopping to a nearby town, and was about to climb up some steps to go into a large store. Coming down the steps was an elderly man clasping three big bunches of flowers. The flowers looked stunning and included lots of red roses. As they passed, Penny said to

the man: 'Oh, somebody's going to be very lucky!' But the man didn't respond in the way she'd expected. Instead, his eyes welled up, and he replied that he was taking them to his wife's grave. She had died some eight months previously. They'd been married for over 60 years, and he was still torn apart by the grief of her loss. As he spoke, the tears began to fall down his face, to such an extent that they splattered onto the ground below.

Instinctively, Penny took the man to one side and gave him a big hug. But it was much more than a hug. It was a meeting of spirits. For a few moments, nothing else existed around them. And through that hug, Penny was able to convey the love, the compassion and the presence of God. It didn't need a speech, a sermon, or a prayer said out loud. No, just a simple hug. And presently, the two of them went on their respective ways, with Penny vowing that she would pray for the man over the coming weeks.

At any given moment, in any given place, there will be lots of folk milling around struggling under the weight of their personal burdens. Some will be fixed inside their own personal bubble, enveloped by their suffering. Others may be longing to off-load their grief to anyone willing to listen.

The Bible gives us the famous tale of 'The Good Samaritan' (Luke 10:30–37), and Penny's story shows how we can all be modern day 'Good Samaritans' if we take the time and trouble to look out for one another. To help others as we ourselves would like to be helped in the same situation. To allow God to flow through us so that we can respond in the right way at the right time. And if we can do that, we will help to spread God's love into our world whenever and wherever it's most needed ... .

A new command I give to you: Love one another. As I have loved you, so you must love one another.   (John 13:34)

Carry each other's burdens ... . (Galatians 6:2a)

Be kind and compassionate to one another ... .
(Ephesians 4:32a)

Who Should Really Be Kept in Cages?

I like most human beings. I know they lack feathers and their noses are a poor apology for a splendid beak, but I have to like them because my owner is one. And we understand one another. If I bow my head, he knows I want a tickle. And if I roll over, he knows I want to lie in the palm of his hand. And if I do a certain call, he knows I want a bath. So I guess we have a special relationship.

So often, as I sit on my perch gazing out of the window at the wild birds and animals, I wish it could be the same for them. I wish they all existed in a world in which there was harmony between human beings and the rest of nature. Because we are all God's creatures experiencing life together. We have all been crafted by the same loving Creator. But sadly, it doesn't seem to work that way. Some humans destroy everything, even when it isn't in their interests to do so. Think of the Amazon Rainforest where a lot of my cousins live. Some 70% of the plants with anti-cancer properties exist only in the Amazon. Quinine for treating Malaria and Turbocuarine for treating Parkinson's Disease and Multiple Sclerosis are derived from Amazonian plants. So what do humans do? They cut down 78 million acres of rainforest every single year (or around 150 acres every minute, every day).

And what about pollinating bees? Humans know that they play a crucial role for the survival of all animal-life on the planet. But many millions die every year around the world because of the way humans use pesticides. And just look at the seas. We all know how important they are for cleansing and providing fish.

But humans poison and pollute them with rubbish, and then overfish out of pure greed.

The crazy thing is that we are all in this world together. We all live in 'God's Garden'. So why do some humans spend all of their time breaking it, trashing it, destroying it, poisoning it, killing, murdering and eradicating its lifeforms? Because humans are destroying it for all of us, themselves included.

Parrots have a very old saying which goes like this:

'No wise parrot gnaws the perch on which it likes to sit'.

If humans carry on destroying this world at their present rate, the whole of creation will come crashing down to earth in a trillion broken pieces. And then it might be too late for them to learn the meaning of words such as 'cherish', 'value', 'respect', 'honour', 'revere', 'share', and 'protect'. Who should really be kept in cages? Parrots or humans?

The Lord God took the man and put him in the Garden of Eden to work it and take care of it.   (Genesis 2:15)

Why Be Alarmed?

One of my favourite party tricks is to imitate the alarm clock. Not the current one, or the one before that, but the alarm clock that my human family used about 12 years ago. If I don't think that my family's up by a reasonable hour, I give a loud blast of 'beep, beep, beep, beep, beep, beep, beep' which usually stirs them into action.

Parrots don't use alarm clocks. We simply follow our natural diurnal rhythm. We awaken when the sun rises, and we go to sleep when it gets dark. Humans like to be different. They invented the alarm clock in the 18th century to give them control over time.

Yes, humans can be very clever, or so they think. But out of all of the inventions they've come up with for their daily lives, the alarm clock is probably the most universally despised. The very name says it all. 'Alarm' clock. Not 'waking' clock. Alarm is a word linked to fear, worry, anxiety and danger. Do humans really want to confront all that as soon as they awaken in the morning?

Some alarm clocks make a loud buzzing sound. Some scream. Some mobile phone alarms mimic the evacuation siren of the sinking Titanic. Meanwhile, an Indian inventor has come up with an alarm clock that gives the sleeper an electric shock if they dare to press the snooze button. And there's even a Japanese alarm clock that sprays water all over your bed if you don't turn it off quickly enough.

So it's really not surprising that a lot of humans wake up feeling unhappy! Maybe, one day in the future, a human will invent an alarm clock that gently stirs the slumbering soul with a gentle Taize chant, a Celtic blessing, or a joyous passage from the Bible. Because an early morning message of love, hope and joy should set us all up for the very best of days . . . .

Shout for joy to the Lord, all the earth.
Worship the Lord with gladness;
    come before Him with joyful songs.
Know that the Lord is God.
    It is He who made us, and we are His;
    We are His people, the sheep of His pasture.

Enter His gates with thanksgiving
    and His courts with praise;
    give thanks to Him and praise His name.
For the Lord is good and His love endures for ever;
    His faithfulness continues through all generations.
                    (Psalm 100)

Wise Parrot, or 'Floored' Parrot?

Some time ago, I quoted an old parrot saying which goes like this:

'A wise parrot never gnaws the perch on which it likes to sit'.

And I'm ashamed to admit that I don't always practise what I preach. I literally came within a millimetre of crashing down to the floor of my cage because I couldn't control my gnawing. And although I'm a parrot, you could say this makes me 'human'. Because if we always believe that we practise what we preach, then we're deceiving ourselves. That applies to vicars and teachers, to judges and politicians – to absolutely all of us. So often we mean well, we aim to say 'the right thing', but we don't always abide by it.

You attract WHAT YOU ARE. If you want "BETTER" be better.

And it's only when we come to terms with our own flaws and failings that we can learn true humility.

And in the same sort of way, it's all too easy for us to believe that we know better than others; that we are wiser and would always do a better job in the same situation. Now that many countries are passing through the peak of the Coronavirus pandemic, some humans are pointing the finger at their politicians and leaders for not having protected them better. And there are also some Presidents who are criticising the World Health Organisation to deflect attention away from their own failings. And while it's always important to ask questions and to learn how to do things better, blunt accusations and finger pointing belong to a culture of blame. The humans that practise this have not yet learnt one of life's basic lessons. For humility serves as the counterweight to hypocrisy. It helps to keep us in check. And it also makes us more receptive to God. Working together is far more effective than creating division.

Jesus had many run-ins with the Pharisees and Sadducees and Teachers of the Law. And somehow, while keeping to the path of humility, He was able to expose them for what they really were. We should all take heed of that.

I've now been given a new perch to replace my old one. I expect that over the coming weeks, I'll gnaw through that one as well. I'll be foolish. But I'll confess my foolishness to God and know that He will still love me for who and what I am ....

Do not judge, and you will not be judged. Do not condemn, and you will not be condemned. Forgive, and you will be forgiven.   (Luke 6:37)

Why do you look at the speck of sawdust in your brother's eye and pay no attention to the plank in your own eye?   (Luke: 6:41)

If any one of you is without sin, let him be the first to throw a stone at her.   (John: 8:7b)

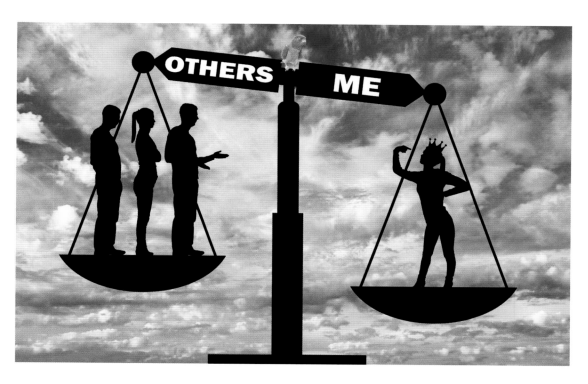

Working to Live or Living to Work?

In many ways, parrots have it made. Because unlike humans, we don't have to go out to work. (In our world, we just help ourselves to whatever happens to be within reach of our beaks.) So no bills or mortgages to worry about; we can be 100% parrot in the way we live out our lives.

And this makes me feel very sorry for humans. I recently heard one complaining that Friday was so close to Monday, and yet Monday seemed so far away from Friday. He clearly didn't enjoy going off to work.

Humans have made their world extremely complex. And sometimes, I find myself asking the question whether 'humans work to live, or do they live to work'? And I suppose that the answer to that question depends upon the type of work they are doing, and the way they choose to approach it. Does their work make them a better person, or does it enable them to help others? Or is their whole working life driven by their need or desire for money?

Let's think about Jesus. During His final three years, He certainly had a lot of work to do. But all the work He undertook was for the benefit of others. For all humanity and Creation. It had nothing to do with money or paying bills. Jesus worked to give everyone a meaningful existence and a long-term future.

Lots of humans can take a leaf out of Jesus' book. Because no job should simply be about the money involved. The common good of humanity and creation needs to be at the heart of what we do in life. And when it is, Monday can seem very close to Friday. Because work takes on a new purpose and meaning.

When humans work only for the sake of money and all that it brings, then they are turning themselves into cage birds. Far bigger cage birds than any parrot or budgie that I know. Money, for money's sake will trap, ensnare, distort and dissatisfy.

My world is very simple in comparison. But who's the 'clever boy' here; me or them?

Whatever you do, work at it with all your heart, as though you are working for the Lord and not for men. Remember that the Lord will give you as a reward what He has kept for His people. For Christ is the real master you serve.

(Colossians 3:23–24. *Amended for clarity*)

Photo credits